The Resilient Power *of* Purpose

7 STEPS TO OWN YOUR DREAM

Larry DiAngi

The Resilient Power of Purpose
7 Steps To Own Your Dream

www.larrydiangi.com
Larry DiAngi Productions
P. O. Box 9056
Erie, PA 16505
Phone (814) 835-9056

Printed in the United States of America

*Dedicated to the memory
of my mom, who believed
in me when I didn't
believe in myself*

Table of Contents

1. Be Propelled by Your Purpose 7

2. Discover Your True Identity 21

3. Expand Your Expectations 37

4. Get In The Presence of Great People — Avoid
   Low-flying People 57

5. Feed Your Power Source Constantly 69

6. Do Things You've Never Done 81

7. Hold The Vision — Know You Were
   Born To Soar 91

Chapter

1

Be Propelled by Your Purpose

"There is no road to success but through a clear strong purpose — nothing can take its place — a purpose underlies character, culture, position, attainment of every sort."
T. T. Munger

"Have a purpose in life, and, having it, throw such strength of mind and muscle into your work as God has given you."
Carlyle

"Ask, and you will receive; seek, and you will find; knock, and it will be opened unto you."
Matthew 7:7

THE REAL YOU

Love	Being
Security	Attracting
Unlimited	Giving
Peace	Flowing
Freedom	True Identity
Faith	Inspired
Worthy	Acting
Indestructible	

THE DRIVER
The real you uses the outer self as
the vehicle of expression.

8

The Outer Self

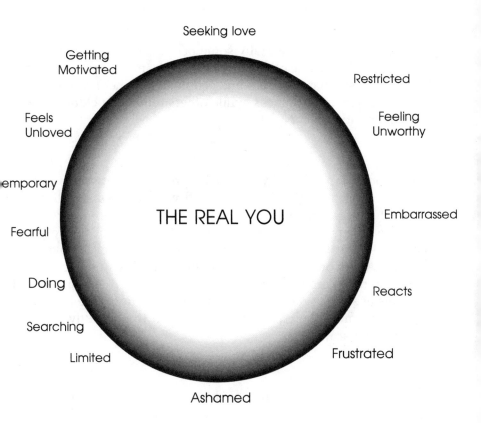

Seeking love

Getting
Motivated

Restricted

Feels
Unloved

Feeling
Unworthy

emporary

THE REAL YOU

Embarrassed

Fearful

Doing

Reacts

Searching

Limited

Frustrated

Ashamed

THE VEHICLE

The outer self becomes the
imposter when you are not
living from the real you.

Be Purpose Driven

Have you ever wondered why some people are able to make their dreams a reality, while others' hopes and dreams remain only a fantasy? What is it that propels some people to a higher level of fulfillment, lifestyle, or happiness, while others remain stuck on a lower level their entire lives?

Many books, tapes, and live seminars promise what seems to be a "quick fix" or a magic pill to make all your dreams a reality and solve all your problems. We all have experienced temporary motivation, which is present one moment and gone the next. We know there must be something more than what the latest self-help fad has to offer. All of our searching for a solution brings us back to the point where we are ready to go beyond short-lived and superficial attempts at staying motivated. What we begin to realize is that we need much more than a temporary solution to get motivated. We need to **be inspired**.

Motivation is simply the natural by-product of inspiration. When you are inspired, you are on a real quest and you are going somewhere wonderful. **All of life changes with the knowledge that you are going somewhere.** If you knew you were leaving tomorrow on an all-expense-paid, two-week vacation to Hawaii, you would probably be in a great mood. The challenges of the day would simply be steps taken in order to get closer to Hawaii. Staying up and packing until one or two o'clock in the morning may not even seem like an inconvenience. In fact, you might be so excited that you can't sleep anyway. You may not enjoy getting up at five a.m. usually, but on this morning, you wake up before your alarm. The difference on this day is that you know you are going somewhere wonderful. When the real you is inspired, motivation comes naturally. Life is not meant to be a boring treadmill on which you are stuck, awaking everyday to fulfill obligations, then falling wearily back into bed, only to get up the next day to go through the same hopeless routine again. When life seems to be lacking purpose, you can either fill your days with enough diversions to distract you from the gnawing ache of emptiness in your heart, or you can set out on a quest for a higher level.

Although your dreams for the higher level in life may include benefits such as more satisfying relationships, financial independence, or greater spiritual, mental, or physical strength, our dreams do not become a reality by merely aspiring for these benefits. **Success comes from becoming truly inspired deep within.** This vision and purpose become the driving force in life, enabling you to go beyond the point of no return. Every person who creates something wonderful starts with a dream. The diagrams at the beginning of this chapter show the difference between the real you and your outer self. A dream that only exists in the outer self simply remains a fantasy, but a dream that lives in the real you becomes your **dream-purpose.** When your dream becomes your purpose, it is no longer optional.

The Real You Versus Outer Self

Learning how to discover your purpose and make your dreams come true is a major premise of this book. But in order to make this happen, you must understand the difference between the real you and the outer self. (2 Corinthians 4:16). Looking at the two diagrams you can see the contrast. The real you is full of love, security, peace, generosity, inspiration, worthiness, and all the other positive quali-

11

ties you possess. The outer self, however, includes qualities such as shame, feelings of unworthiness, frustration, insecurity and fear. The real you is supposed to be the driver who uses the outer self as the vehicle of expression. Your outer self becomes an imposter when you are not living from who you really are. The real you possesses everything you need to make your dreams come true, you just need to begin living life from the inside out. By doing so, you will move to higher and higher levels until you reach your dream. As a plane taxis down the runway, there is a point at which it has used up too much of the runway and built up too much thrust and too much lift to abort the mission; it must take-off and fly. There is something similar that happens in our lives when we step over that line. Going forward to the next level is no longer simply an option or something to do only if it's convenient. We **know** the next level has our name on it.

Many people spend their entire lives just taxiing around the runway. They never really take off and fly and they never really step over that line. Rather than moving beyond the point of no return, they always leave a way to escape. But when you finally step over that line, the magic begins. Charisma exudes from you. The right people come into your life and you always seem to be at the right place at the right time. We may not always understand how or why life works this way — it just does.

More important than what you want in life is why you want what you want in life. The why is where the power is. The **why** is what causes you to **go beyond the point of no return.** The why is your purpose in life. I remember a story about two young boys, eight and nine years old. They were playing on a frozen pond in their neighborhood. As they played, they skipped, jumped, threw snowballs, and did all the things young boys do to have fun on a cold winter day. All of a sudden, the nine-year-old boy turned around to see his friend fall through a thin spot in the ice to the cold depths below. The piece of ice that broke came up and shut the hole like a trap door. On impulse, the nine-year-old ran over to a tree, grabbed a three-inch-thick branch, and ripped it off the tree. He ran to the spot where his friend had fallen through and began to beat the ice until, finally, he broke a hole eight feet wide. He found the hood of his friend's parka and pulled him up to safety.

Soon the ambulance arrived and the paramedics checked the young boy's vital signs. They wrapped blankets around the boy and gave him hot chocolate. Once it was announced that he was going to be fine, the crowd began to buzz. People started looking at the branch, which was over three inches thick. They started looking at the ice that was broken and noticed that, in some places, it was several inches thick. They started asking questions like, "How could such a young boy break this branch? Nine-year-olds can't break branches this thick! And how could such a young boy break this ice? It's too thick for a nine-year-old to break!"

None of the answers they could come up with to these questions seemed to make sense, though. Then a hush came over the crowd and an elderly gentleman, with gray streaking through his hair, came from the back of the crowd and said, "I can tell you why this young boy could break this branch and ice. He did it because *there was no one here to tell him it was impossible.*" This gentleman understood that the boy's purpose was so big, and the love for his friend was so great, that he did not bother to measure the branch to see if he would be able to break it. Love for his friend drove him over to that tree. Even if he could not break the branch, he had to go ahead and attempt it anyway. Even if he wasn't strong enough to break the ice, he had to attempt to break it anyway. Why? Because the purpose driving him was overwhelming.

Discover Your Purpose

What is the purpose driving your life? Why do you want to move to your next level? A higher level in your life might involve loving and supporting your family. It might involve becoming a stronger person and providing a service that will help others. Your purpose might be to achieve financial freedom. You don't just want the money, but the freedom that accompanies financial security. You understand there is almost nothing worse than financial bondage, and you want to be free to live life on your own terms.

You were meant to have not only what you need to live a wonderful life and to enjoy all the things that God put on Earth, but also to have more than what you need so you are able to give some of your abundance away. Only then can you obey the law of reciprocity, which states that if you give, more will be given to you. However, if you are not prospering spiritually, mentally, emotionally, or financially, then giving becomes very difficult.

What is the rationale for what you want? Purpose-driven people go beyond the point of no return. They are people who have **stepped over a line,** and they know some things for certain which they once only understood. You can understand the need to live with a strong sense of purpose. You can even acknowledge that the rationale for striving for something better is more important than the facts that challenge your higher level, but if you do not have a strong enough purpose, then you will probably never get to a higher level because your reasons for what you want are so small that just about anything will stop you.

When doubts, fears, or feelings of inferiority come into your life, you can use your sense of purpose to overcome negativity and propel you past your fears. I am not just talking about thinking positively in a superficial sense. A true positive attitude comes because you know something. Although you understand many important things in life, you need to go beyond a shallow understanding and begin to **know** them.

Understanding Versus Knowing

An example from my own life illustrates the distinction between understanding and knowing. I was conducting a workshop, as I have many times, and broke the crowd into groups of six or eight people. I then gave each group a process and exercise. I knew if it took a minute for each person to complete the exercise, and there were six to eight people around the table, then I had approximately eight minutes free to leave the room. So I left to get a drink of water and use the restroom. When I was finished, I walked into the seminar room and back up to the podium. As I walked to the front, I noticed it was very silent — everybody was just looking at me. I thought, *Wow, these principles must be making a real impact on these folks.* But then I thought, *Wait a minute. These people are supposed to be doing an exercise and talking to each other What's going on here ?*

Well, I shrugged it off, as I have had to do many times as a speaker in order to remain focused, and concluded the workshop. After the workshop, a woman came up to my table to purchase some tapes. She said, "Larry, I really enjoyed your workshop. It was tremendous. But can I tell you something?" "Sure!" I replied. She proceeded, "You know that cordless microphone you are wearing? You have to shut those off before you use the restroom." I did not want to know any more. She had already given me more than enough information to make me blush, but she continued to talk. "Larry, we were right in the middle of that exercise you had set up beautifully. We were working through the principle perfectly, and then, all of a sudden, we heard a toilet flush over the speakers." I was so glad I did not take that opportunity to sing as I have at other times.

I have been speaking in front of crowds for over twenty years, and in that period of time I have used every type of microphone conceivable. Microphones with and without cords, hand-held microphones, and cordless lapel microphones like I was wearing that day. Until then, I understood that you do not have a private conversation with the microphone turned on, and you certainly never use the restroom without shutting it off. But now I do not just understand that concept, **I know it.**

A couple of weeks ago, I was conducting a workshop when the same thing happened. I walked out of the room in the middle of the workshop to use the restroom. With the aforementioned experience fresh on my mind, something deep within me cried out, *Larry, shut your microphone off!* As a result, I was able to avoid embarrassment on that occasion.

You see, I once understood something, but now I know it. Many times it takes a conscious shock to bring you back to a place of knowing, and there is a way for you to maintain that sense of knowing. I am going to talk about that in this book. The approach that many people take to get to a higher level and to realize their dreams is ineffective because they do not know the true purpose which supports their dreams. In Scripture, Romans 8:28 says, "And we <u>know</u> that all things work together for good to them that love God, to them who are called according to His purpose." Knowing that, "All things will work together for your good." and that this is part of God's purpose for your life, is something that you can only know deep inside you. There is a tendency in life to try to manipulate qualities that exist in your outer self in order to move to a higher level, but this manipulation fails to move you higher. The real you is on the inside. The apostle Paul states in 2 Corinthians 4:16, "For which cause we faint not; but though our outward man perish, yet the inward man is renewed day by day." This "inward man" is the "real you." The real you is where your purpose lives, and where you draw the strength to overcome the fears and doubts that come against you and prohibit you from reaching your dreams. The outer self is simply a vehicle you use to manifest your dreams. You drive in a car, but you are not the car. You fly in a plane, you are not the plane. You walk around in a body, you are not your body. As you see in the two diagrams at the beginning of this chapter, you "flow" in your God given purpose from the real you. From your outer self, you "struggle" and try to force things to happen. From the real you, you "attract" what you need and desire in life. From your outer self you try to "get." People who live totally in their outer selves have the philosophy, "get all you can, can all you get, and sit on the can." From the real you, you are not struggling to get things. You know that receiving the best in life is what you are truly worthy of and that turning your dreams into a reality is part of God's purpose for your life.

Learn To Get Focused

I will talk throughout this book about principles and techniques you can use to center yourself on a consistent, continual basis. Centering simply means moving from the outside to the inside to flow from the real you. When you live your dreams, you receive abundance in every single area of life. Spiritual, mental, emotional, physical, and financial abundance are all achieved by flowing in your dream-purpose. When you learn to center yourself, you will make your dreams a reality, reaching higher and higher levels in life. You must learn to become strong on the inside, working daily to make sure you are not just understanding things, but you **know that you know** about the most important things in life.

The real you is the offspring of the creator. The scriptures tell us in Genesis 1:27: "So God created man is his own image. In the image of God created he him; male and female created he them." We are also called the children of God. So logic tells us that the offspring are always like unto their parent. Nature also confirms this as an absolute fact. Rabbits never have monkeys, and eagles never give birth to chickens. Eagles give birth to little baby eaglets. Therefore when God the Creator has children, they are born with creative ability. We are not born to crawl through life like a worm content to live on a lower level. We were born to create a wonderful life for ourselves and help others do the same in their life. You see, that is the truth about **who you really are** on the inside. That is where you are spirit and unlimited. That is where you know you are worthy, and where you feel totally secure, surrounded by love, peace, and purpose. Your outer self includes the physical body, your outer mind, will, and emotions. All of these can be vulnerable to fear and insecurity and can fluctuate according to your circumstances, the weather, other people, and many other influences. It is where you feel unworthy and limited, and where you refuse to believe people love you. You don't even love yourself, because you are not aware of who you really are inside. All of the negative, destructive emotions live on the outside. In the real you there is genuine confidence. On the outside, all you can do is fake confidence, and there is nothing more transparent than artificial confidence. When you feel low emotionally, you will seem weak and your mind will be confused.

You can override the tendency to want to give up on your dream by refocusing yourself and centering yourself back "on purpose."

To fulfill a dream, you must move to a higher level. The outer self, when left to itself, believes it will be totally fulfilled if it acquires prestige, money, and power. The outer self's motivation for moving to a higher level and reaching a dream is to appear successful. The real you's reason for moving to a higher level is your real purpose for getting there. Most dreams on the outside simply stay a dream and never become a reality. In fact, most people never act on their dreams when they are living strictly from their outer selves. This predicament is a result of not attempting to discover their true purpose and real identity.

Chapter

2

Discover Your
True Identity

"Nothing splendid has ever
been achieved except by
those who dared believe
that something inside
of them was superior
to circumstance."
–Bruce Barton

*"For which cause we faint not; but though the outward man perish,
yet the inward man is renewed day by day."*

2 Corinthians 4:16

The Outer Self

Dream-fantasy

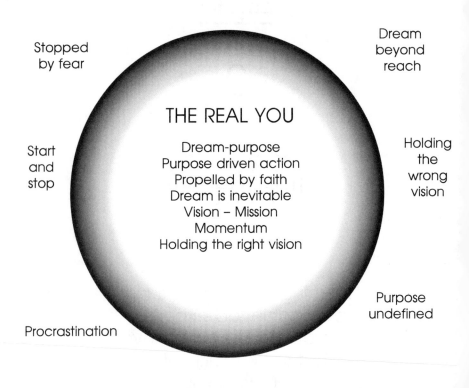

Stopped
by fear

Dream
beyond
reach

THE REAL YOU

Start
and
stop

Dream-purpose
Purpose driven action
Propelled by faith
Dream is inevitable
Vision – Mission
Momentum
Holding the right vision

Holding
the
wrong
vision

Procrastination

Purpose
undefined

When you bring your dream inside, it
becomes your dream-purpose.

Discover Your True identity

Bring Your Dream Inside

As you use the principles and thoughts you find in this book, you will begin to discover the real you and your real purpose. You will be able to take the seemingly unattainable dream that exists in your outer self and bring it inside. Your dream will then become a purpose. When you internalize your dream, it is no longer something you simply wish would happen. You no longer have just a dream-fantasy, you have a **dream-purpose.** You become unstoppable, with the strength of your purpose propelling you to a higher level.

You must assimilate your dreams. Food sitting on a plate is simply food, but when you eat it, it becomes part of you. Principles and dreams are the same way. When they exist outside, they are simply things for which to hope. It is amazing to think of all the people who dream about winning the lottery, but who never even buy a ticket! A dream on the outside is only known to the dreamer, but as you begin to flow from who you really are, then that dream is transformed into a purpose. The real you is indestructible, and everything you need is accessible to you. Abundant life exists within the real you. If you strictly operate from your outer self, then you are in the midst of the struggle. But if you are flowing from who you really are, you are attracting what you need and desire in life. You are also being who you were meant to be. What a great difference there is between struggling and flowing.

Why do you attract good when you live from within? Because the power of your being is on the inside, and all the negative influences are on the outside. The outer self is supposed to be a vehicle. However, the outer self becomes destructive when left to itself. A car without a driver, if it is rolling down the road, will surely crash into something. We are the same way when we are not flowing from who we really are. We receive all kinds of influence, both good and bad, from family, friends, media, and education. How we were reared has a great influence on our outer selves. The list of other influences is almost endless. If we are not flowing from who we really are, then we have created an imposter. The outer self becomes an imposter who talks and acts, but is independent and disconnected from who we really are. It is no surprise that we feel insecure when living only from the outside. We never really feel that we are loved, and we refuse to believe that we can be loved unconditionally.

Why is it that some people make their dreams a reality, achieving financial freedom and experiencing the love of family and friends with more peace and less stress than ever before? Though this scenario sounds like a dream, you can make it a reality. How does that transformation happen? It happens when you live according to your purpose.

Discover Your True Identity

Many problems arise when people believe their identity consists of the outer self — their physical body, fluctuating emotions, limited mind and will power. The outer self is highly impressionable and estimates its self worth based solely on success, failures, profession, place of origin, education, family, outer influences, relationships, and experiences. When you start to believe that these factors make up your identity, then you can never break free of the lower level and move to a higher level. You must know that your present level has nothing to do with your true identity. When you detach yourself from this false identity, then the guilt and insecurity which held you captive loses its grip. You step back, perhaps for the first time, and think, *Wait a minute. This isn't who I am. All of this stuff is just part of the outer package.* No matter how amazing the outside of a birthday present looks, the contents are more important than the wrapping paper and bows.

Each of us was born for a great purpose. You need to know that you were not born to struggle. You were not born to live on a lower level, but to move continuously to higher levels. Your outer dream becomes an inner purpose. The real you will naturally say, "I know I am wired to be prosperous. I am made in the image and likeness of God. I am the offspring of the Creator. Therefore, **I was born to create, succeed, and prosper. I was born to move to higher levels. I was born to turn my dreams into reality.**"

The outer self is not wired to succeed and is never really happy. Even if the outer self seems to turn a dream into reality, it is never really fulfilled. It is always reaching for the next thing because it is never satisfied. You were wired to live according to who you really are. The offspring of the Creator must be creative, vibrant, and spiritually indestructible.

I remember going to a garage sale and finding a table saw for twenty dollars. I thought, *Wow, what a deal! A table saw for $20!!* I looked it over and realized that the only thing wrong was that the power plug was missing from the end of the cord. I asked the man who was running the sale, "Does this saw work?" He said, "Yes, it does.

It works great." "Are you sure it works?" I asked. "There is no plug on the end of the cord." "Yes," he said, "I've used it myself and it works great. I broke the plug off as I was moving things around for the sale today, and I don't know where it is. I lost it." I said OK and gave him the twenty dollars, put the saw in my car, and took it home.

When I got home, I put another plug on the end of the cord and plugged it in the wall. I flipped on the table saw and it buzzed a little bit and hummed, and then it just quit. I thought, *Wow, it looks like maybe this doesn't work after all.* Then I did what most people do as a last resort and read the instructions on the back! I discovered I had put the wrong type of plug on the end of the cord and had plugged it into a 110 volt electrical outlet. The instruction plate on the back of the saw clearly stated that this saw ran on 220 volts. With some help from my dad I attached the proper plug and plugged it into a 220 volt electrical outlet. With the right amount of power that table saw cut wood like a hot knife through butter.

Many people are the same way — trying to run on less power than intended. You were not wired to fail or settle for existing on a lower level than you desire. You were born to make your dream a reality by moving to higher levels your entire life. It is a shame but many people die from boredom very young in life, even though the physical body still lives on for many years. You were not born to live the same life as everyone else, day after day. Rather, there is a deep calling within us all. **That inner knowing, that inner hunger, that inner sense that your dream and your next level are waiting for you is the voice of your purpose speaking to you.** Listen to it, and begin to flow from who you really are.

About nine years ago, I was at a point in my life where I had leveled off and peaked out. I had made a decision by not making any decisions in my life. I had made a decision not to make waves or to break out of my comfort zone and reach for a higher level. I had gone on for quite some time with the knowledge that there was another place for me to go and another level on which to operate. By that point, I had worked in a number of different areas. At age sixteen, I played drums in different rock bands. Then I got a job as a shop worker on an assembly line, but realized that was not for me. I moved on to sell fire extinguishers, and then moved on to be the sales director for a local magazine. I spent some time working in the ministry and enjoyed my time as a counselor working with juvenile delinquents. I had come to a place in my life where I was speaking to groups of people and sharing different principles on a regular basis. At this time, I achieved the dream I had to be on television. I had a weekly half-hour program on an ABC affiliate, as well as a radio program on weekdays. I seemed to have reached a lot of my goals, and was enjoying a lot of the things I thought were going to fulfill me. There are signs all along the road of life that say **NO PARKING HERE**, but I had parked. I had decided I was going to ride out the wave, and that I was not really in the mood to climb another mountain.

I went on for a period of time ignoring that inner prompting to move towards a higher level. Through refusing to move on and set my sights higher, I had begun to live on the outside and merely enjoy all the things of life. The bills were being paid, although I did not have a lot of extra money, it gave me a certain sense of security to realize I looked fine to others. Eventually, the thought that I was merely existing and not being completely myself caught up with me. I developed a headache that lasted twenty-nine days. I remember walking into my office, sitting behind my desk, putting my face into my hands, and realizing I had had a non-stop headache for twenty-nine days. I had tried aspirin, but it became very clear to me that my headache was not the result of an aspirin deficiency. I went to doctors who gave me prescription painkillers, but none of them would touch my headache. I woke up with a headache, lived all day with a headache, went to bed with a headache, and woke up in the middle of the night with a headache. It was there to remind me something was wrong. On the twenty-ninth day I remember thinking, *God, I realize this headache is not simply a physical situation, but a physical symptom coming from a deep ache in my heart. I ache because I refuse to move up higher. God, if you open the door, I'll go through it. Just point me in the right direction.*

A Serendipitous Encounter

I had a speaking engagement in Pittsburgh, Pennsylvania the next day. After driving there and speaking, I visited a couple of friends who lived in that area. As I was getting ready to leave, one friend handed me a tape and said, "Larry, listen to this tape. Have you ever heard of this fellow, Les Brown?" "No," I said, "I've never heard of him." He said, "Well, you'll really enjoy this tape — listen to it." So I left the house and, as I drove home, I popped the tape into the tape deck and began to listen.

Something began to stir within me. As I listened, Les' words inspired me and new hope began to well up inside my heart. I could hear from the tape the sound of thousands of people in his audience clapping and responding with a thunderous roar at different points as he spoke. I realized that Les Brown was really a great speaker. But more than that, I knew that Les and I were supposed to be working together. Today Les Brown is a house hold name because of his Emmy-Award winning PBS specials, nationally syndicated talkshow, and best selling books. But, since I had not yet heard of Les, I had to figure out where and how to contact him. On the tape

I heard him say that he lived in Detroit, Michigan, so, I called information and got his office phone number. The next day I woke up and called Les' office. He was out of town, so I left a message with the receptionist. I figured it would make a greater impact if I left a few messages that day, so I called a couple more times. The next day, I woke up and left ten more messages. I called every day for six weeks, between ten and fifteen times a day. Little did I know, the staff in Les' office assumed I was some kind of crazy man and stopped giving Les the messages after the first couple of days. Seven days a week for six weeks I called ten to fifteen times a day. I would even call on Saturdays and Sundays and leave messages with the answering service. I knew this was the direction I was supposed to go in, and that working with Les had everything to do with my next level. You never go alone to the next level in life. There is always someone helping you, and there are always people who you will help along the way. But, remember, **the most important people that will help you pursue your dream may be people you haven't met yet!!**

It was 6:30 p.m. on a Tuesday night, six weeks later, when I dialed that phone number one more time to Les Brown's office. Les had just returned from a trip and was sitting in his office returning phone calls. Normally, the staff would reroute four of the five phone lines in the office to an answering service. The fifth line was a private number that only a few people knew, and that line was left open at all times for direct calls. It was more than just a coincidence, I believe, that this night the staff forgot to reroute those four phone lines. I dialed the phone and it rang through. Les, thinking it was the private line, picked up the phone and said hello. I said, "Hello, who is this?" He said, "Les Brown. Who is this?" "This is Larry DiAngi," I replied. "Do I know you, Larry?" he asked. I answered, "Well, my name probably sounds familiar. I have left a lot of messages at your office in the last few weeks." He said, "No, I don't recognize it. It might sound a little familiar, but no, not really." At that point, I thought to myself, *oh my. After 500 messages he doesn't ' even recognize my name!* So I mustered up strength and said, "Well, I don't know about that, but what I do know, Les, is that you and I are going to be working together." He said, "Well, Larry, you know it's very kind of you to call. I'm flattered you would consider me, but I have twenty or thirty people calling every week who want to work with me." So I said, "Well, Les, I don't know about that either, but..." and I continued to talk. After ten minutes, there was something that shifted in our conversation, an immediate bond took place and we both knew that we had just discovered a brother that we never knew we had. Les said, "Larry, I don't believe this, but I know that what you are saying is true. Can you get to Detroit tomorrow so we can meet and talk?" "Certainly," I said, and jumped on a plane to Detroit on the first flight the next morning.

I took a taxi to Les' office building and arrived there at 9:45 a.m. I had an appointment to meet with Les at 10:00 a.m. The elevators were broken, and Les' office was on the twenty-first floor, so I sat downstairs in the cafeteria and drank coffee for about an hour. Suddenly, I made up my mind to walk up the twenty-one floors, as the building security guards told me the elevators were out indefinitely. My purpose was so big that twenty-one flights were not going to stop me.

After walking up the stairs, I was sweating profusely. I went into one of the restrooms, splashed some cold water on my face, and proceeded to walk in and meet Les. We sat down for lunch and talked over a number of wonderful strategies about how we were going to do all kinds of great things together. I left with the agreement that I would return to Detroit the following Wednesday to have lunch and we would spend a few hours together again.

The following week, I flew back and we spent more time discussing different ways we could work together in the speaking business. Finally, Les turned to me and said, "Larry, I have to go catch a plane. I'm flying to Phoenix to conduct a workshop for some doctors there." I said OK, and he said, "Larry, this is wonderful. We are going to do some great things. I'm so excited." I began to walk out of the office door, when I suddenly felt compelled to ask him if I could go to Phoenix with him. He said, "Well, I guess you can. But my plane leaves in 45 minutes and you don't have a ticket." I said, "Don't worry about it." I ran to the phone, dialed Northwest Airlines, and asked them if there was an available seat to Phoenix from Detroit on Les' flight. They said, "Yes, we do have a seat, but the plane leaves in 35 or 40 minutes. How far are you from the airport?" I said, "I can get there. How much is the ticket?" The woman on the phone replied, "That will be $790 sir." At that moment, I realized I did not have any money. I had a credit card in my pocket, but I was sure that my available credit was not high enough. I gave the credit card number anyway and, miraculously, it went through and my reservation was confirmed. We jumped in the car, drove to the airport, got the ticket, jumped on the plane, and flew to Phoenix. When we picked up our baggage, a limousine met us outside and we drove to the Ritz Carlton Hotel. After stepping out of the limousine, we walked into the spacious marble lobby, and I immediately remembered I was broke. As we started walking towards the front desk, Les looked at me and said, "Larry, you know what? We have a lot of things to talk about. We still have some strategies to work out for what we are going to do in the future. Why don't I just get a room with two double beds and we'll bunk together tonight? That way, we'll have some time to talk." Even though I was trembling inside, wondering how I was going to pay for a room, I looked over at Les and very calmly said, "Yes, Les. That sounds great."

We talked for a while and both became very tired because it was late. Les climbed into his bed and I climbed into mine. Just as I was about to drift off to sleep, Les said, "Larry, I'll tell you what. Why don't you take an hour tomorrow and speak to these doctors. I have a six-hour workshop. I'll start it out, you can talk for an hour and a half, then I'll finish it up." I said, "Les, you have never heard me speak before. If I don't do a good job, it will reflect on you. By the way, how much are they paying you for this seminar tomorrow?" At that time, for a full day, his fee was $7,500. I said, "For that much money, they're going to be really mad if I don't do well!" He replied, "Larry, don't worry about it. You'll do great."

In the two weeks since I realized this was the new level on which I was supposed to operate, I had been up late every night preparing new material. I had a file folder in my briefcase with little scraps of paper, as well as napkins and legal pads, on which I had scribbled notes. I grabbed that file folder, got out of bed, went into the bathroom, and spent the majority of that night in the bathroom preparing a talk to share with the doctors. About an hour before it was time to get up, I emerged from the bathroom to get a little rest.

When the alarm went off, Les and I got up, got dressed, and went down to the ballroom where the doctors had gathered. Les started the seminar, spoke for an hour and a half, then pointed to the back of the room and said, "Now I would like to introduce one of the greatest speakers in America, Larry DiAngi." I looked behind me to see who he was talking about, and then realized I needed to start walking toward the front of the room. I walked up, took the microphone, opened my mouth, and it felt as if I was outside of my body, watching myself give the presentation. Those doctors were on the edge of their seats taking notes as fast as they could. A new Larry was born that day. My headache left and, within two weeks, I was living in Detroit. Les became my mentor and my brother and we joined forces to pursue our dreams. I was beginning to live on my higher level.

We all have things we would like to happen in our lives, things we can imagine accomplishing or experiencing. These areas of life may be physical, mental, emotional, spiritual, or financial. While the first step to making your dreams come true is acknowledging that you have a dream for what you want to happen, it remains only a wish or fantasy if you take it no farther than that first thought. It is possible to live your entire life thinking about all the things you would like to do or make happen without any of them becoming your reality. Without **purpose-driven action,** your wishes will never come to fruition. This concept is illustrated in the diagram. **Every person who has ever created something great starts with an idea or a dream.** At the beginning of this chapter, we learned that a dream located in the outer self simply remains a fantasy. When you begin to flow from the real you and devote time to look honestly at your ideas and determine the exact steps you will need to take to achieve what you desire, your dream will become a reality to you on the inside even before it is manifested on the outside. Once your dream becomes a reality to you on the inside, action is automatic because you realize it already belongs to you and you begin pursuing your dream with a passion.

When you bring your dream into the real you, it becomes your dream-purpose and great things will happen in your life. You will begin to meet the right people and find the right opportunities. The right thoughts combined with purpose-driven action propel you upward toward your higher level. With the help of your daily program of inspirational and motivational books, tapes, music, and social interaction, you can create positive changes in your thought process and, in turn, you will be driven to act rather than procrastinate. You will begin to **own your dream!**

Your Dream Is Included In The Price of The Ticket

There was a young man who boarded an ocean liner to travel abroad. He handed the attendant his ticket and went straight to his room, carrying a suitcase in one hand and a large brown bag in the other. After entering his room, he shut the door. He put his suitcase on the bed and the large brown bag on the table. From the bag he removed three large jars of peanut butter and several large boxes of crackers. As he looked at them, he thought to himself, I *had just enough money to buy the ticket to board this ship, but not enough money to buy food in the dining room, so I guess this will be my diet for the next two weeks.*

For the next two weeks, the man only ventured out of his room a few times to get some fresh air. He did not want to talk to the other passengers because he was ashamed he could not afford to eat with the other guests. At the end of the voyage as he was getting off the ship, the captain stopped him and said, "Hello Sir. I don't believe I've met you. I usually try to shake hands and greet all the guests at least once in the dining room, but I did not see you. I know that some people do not travel well on water. I hope you did not experience sea sickness during our voyage." The man responded timidly, "No, I kept to myself during this trip because I was ashamed that I had no money to buy food in your dining room after spending it all on my ticket." With regret, the captain informed him, "Sir, I wish you had mentioned this to me earlier. You see, all meals are included in the price of each ticket we sell for this ocean liner."

What a tragedy that so many people do not realize their dream is included in the price of each ticket in life! The mere fact that you are alive means **your dream is included in the ticket that brought you here.** And the fact that you have a dream means it already belongs to you. You just need to apply the **right foundational principles** with **constant action** long enough to see your dream manifested.

Be a purpose-driven person, discover your true identity, constantly expand your expectations, place yourself in the presence of great people and, when in their presence, duplicate their success with relentless action. Feed your power source constantly, be willing to do things you've never done, and hold the vision. If you follow all of these steps, **you will be absolutely unstoppable.** You will begin to see your life in terms of when you will make your dream a tangible reality rather than if you will make your dream a reality.

The process of making your dream happen can be compared to fission. There is power trapped inside the nucleus of a uranium atom which cannot be released without applying the right principles. The nucleus is surrounded by a negative electron cloud, which is very strong. A neutron beam must be used to break through the electron cloud and penetrate the nucleus.

In the same way, you must apply principles for success with relentless action until you break out of the outer self and into the real you. Only then will you begin to realize your dream. The wonderful thing, though, is that the real you and your dream are inseparable. When you work on one, you automatically work on the other. As you work on yourself and your dream everyday, there will be times when you wonder whether any progress is being made. That is the time to turn up the heat like never before.

Right before an atom splits, a strange phenomenon occurs. The nucleus actually depresses and, for a short time, it seems as though all the energy it took to penetrate the negative electron cloud to reach the nucleus was in vain. Then all at once, while still in a depressed state, the nucleus undergoes a total change. The atom splits, incredible energy is released, and a chain reaction occurs affecting the surrounding atoms.

When you have been working on yourself and your dream and nothing seems to be happening, **you may be only a fraction of an inch away from success.** How would you like tremendous energy to be released in your life, affecting you financially, spiritually, mentally, physically, in relationships, and emotionally? For this to occur, you must get through the times when it seems nothing is happening and you feel like quitting. You must go back to the principles that you know work and apply them with more passion than ever before. **This is the time to expend all the energy, time and creativity possible to make your dream a reality.**

As you continue to read this book, you will encounter some principles which will help you flow from the real you in every area of life. **Your purpose is calling you. Please do not settle for any less.**

Chapter

3

Expand Your Expectations

"Success is based on imagination *plus*
ambition *and* the will to work."
—*Thomas Edison*

"For imagination sets the goal "picture"
which our automatic mechanism works on.
We act, or fail to act, not because of "will,"
as is so commonly believed, but
because of imagination."
—*Maxwell Maltz*

The Outer Self

Circumstance-based
expectancy

Thoughts
attract
lower quality
experiences,
relationships
and
opportunities

Distorted
picture of
you created
by history

THE REAL YOU

Purpose-driven expectancy
Accurate picture of your idenity
Positive principle-based self-talk
Unlimited capacity to receive
Superceding laws
Thoughts attract your highest
and best

Negative
outer
influence
based
self-talk

Limited
capacity
to receive

Our capacity to receive is determined
by what we believe we are worthy of.
What we believe we are worthy of is
determined by the picture we have
of ourselves. What we see — is
what we get.

Expand Your Expectations

There is a reliable, constant, irrefutable set of laws and principles governing all of life. At times, it seems as though life is nothing more than a collection of out-of-control events. All of the different areas of life seem to be in a constant state of flux. You wonder at times whether anything in life stays sure and constant; whether anything exists that you can always come back to as a benchmark, a turning point. You do not have to live long to realize that almost everything outside of yourself is unreliable at best. Yet history shows us a consistent stream of people who have taken unsure circumstances, relationships, and opportunities and have built wonderful lives for themselves. These people have molded strong, purpose-filled lives. A person who lives a purpose-filled life will often have a position of influence with friends, acquaintances, and family. They turn adversity and trouble into triumphs, obstacles into opportunities. We watch them use every mountain to gain momentum in pursuing their purpose with a passion.

As you can see in the diagram, living according to the real you produces expectations based on your purpose in life rather than on your circumstances in life. As a result, you become the driver of your own life and are in control and moving toward your dream. The real you thrives on positive affirmations based on superceding principles, and, as a result, has an accurate picture of your self-worth. When the real you is in control, you have an unlimited capacity to receive.

The outer self, represented by the outer circle, feeds on negative thinking when operating independent from the real you. This negativity produces a distorted picture of yourself based on all of the discouraging influences you have known throughout your life. When your outer self is in control, you cannot move toward your dreams because your capacity to receive and flourish is limited. The outer self is always stuck and cannot move past the challenging circumstances of life.

Live According To Solid Principles

People who live purpose-filled lives deal with the same external forces that we all deal with. They face self-doubt, time and energy limitations, and on-going change. Yet they prevail. What makes them different? What causes a person to press forward at all costs, even in the face of adversity and when obstacles seem insurmountable? One of the things that causes people to have this resiliency of spirit is that they come to a place of knowing in life that there is a set of principles to live by that is absolutely reliable. The principles work if you apply them and they work all the time. **They work to the extent that you assimilate them into your life and then live by them.**

One of these principles is that you must constantly expand your expectations because you are a magnet. Proverbs 23:7, states: "As he thinketh in his heart, so is he." In other words, whatever you expect, whatever you think about, whatever you concentrate or meditate on, will become your experience in life. That's what you will receive. We are all magnets, attracting everything we receive in life, both positive and negative.

Metaphorically speaking, we have all had "packages" delivered to the doorway of our life for which we really did not want to sign. We might have said, "Wait a minute, I didn't order that." But there are no accidents. Somehow we focused our magnetic ability to attract what we did not want. We can, however, use our magnetic ability positively to reach the next level of our dream-purpose.

By working with the right benchmark principles, you can pull your next level to you, drawing yourself up higher as a result. **It is extremely vital that you constantly take inventory and reevaluate the principles on which you choose to base your life.** What benchmarks are you relying on that make up the foundation of your inspiration in life? You must always make sure that you are not leaning your ladder up against the wrong wall. A story about two people driving in a car illustrates this point. The passenger, reading a map, turns to the driver and says, "Wait a minute, we're going in the wrong direction. We're going south, but we need to be going north." The driver responds to the passenger by saying, "Well, it's too late now. We can't take the time to turn around, we're making such good time." At times in life you need to slow down and examine yourself, making sure all the activity you are involved in and all the energy you are expending is based on foundational principles and benchmarks that are going to move you in the right direction toward your higher level.

When a person goes to school to become a surveyor, he first learns from books and instructors all about the profession of surveying, or measuring land. After he has learned a certain amount from books and classroom instruction, he is sent out to test his skills as a surveyor. Somewhere on the grounds is a mound of dirt or a block of cement with a brass plaque on top. The brass plaque states the exact elevation at this location. At any point when the student is out measuring land and feels that he has lost his bearings and may not be charting the right course, he can always come back to the brass plaque. Returning to the brass plaque, or benchmark, enables him to start over again with the knowledge that he is starting from a reliable place. Then he will regain a sure footing, a strong foundation, and can begin again to measure the land with a renewed sense of confidence. Life is the same way for you. Many times you feel you are in uncharted territory. You're going for the next level and turning your dream into a purpose. You're working on yourself every single day, making sure that you are not operating from the outside. At times you must return to the benchmark, or, in this case, to your dream-purpose and expectations.

Verbalize Your Expectations

Expanding your expectations is not as simple as just saying you want to do it. However, expanding your expectations does start with saying that you are expanding your expectations. You must first **speak it to yourself** and then to those close to you who form the inner circle of people in whom you have confidence. Make sure you do not share these things with people who are not also on the journey to the next level, because they will not understand and, many times, will try to discourage you.

After you begin to verbalize your expectations, you must also **write them down.** Your expectations must be built on the firm foundation of your purpose in life. A good question to ask yourself is, *Am I acting upon life, or is life acting upon me?* By applying these principles and benchmarks, you will begin to flow from who you really are.

Many of your reasons for wanting certain things in life change when you allow the real you to be in control. Great relationships are wonderful, but you don't want great relationships just to have people around you. You want great relationships that complement you and are consistent with the way you were wired. You are here to give love and to receive love. The exchange that takes place makes life fulfilling and wonderful. Without it, life seems very empty.

Keeping your physical body in shape has many benefits, too. Having a strong, pain-free vehicle in which to operate enhances mental and emotional peace and helps you focus more clearly. When an imbalance exists there, you can lose perspective on life.

Another benefit to living on a higher level is financial independence and prosperity. Financial prosperity does not mean merely making money in order to buy many "things." I remember an interview with Johnny Carson in which the interviewer asked him what all of his fame and wealth had done for him. His reply, which was pretty amazing, was that the most important thing having a lot of money had done for him was eliminate the need to worry about money. What a tremendous concept! Can you imagine a life in which you do not need to worry about having enough money? You could set your mind and heart on being creative, helping people, loving people, and doing the things you believe you are here to do. Money is much more than just paper with pictures of dead presidents on it. Money is an exchange of energy. Most people give the best, most awake, prime time 40, 50, or 60 hours of their week for this thing we call money. We give our energy, creativity, and service in exchange for dollars. When we are trying to get money we are involved in the struggle. When we are in the flow we attract financial prosperity. Man was not born just to make a living, but by living his making, he will attract his living. As you begin to move to your next level, there is greater freedom financially, as well as in every other area of life.

Act, Don't React

You are either acting or reacting in life. If you plan and deliberately apply benchmark principles and superceding laws, then you are acting upon life. If not, then you are simply reacting to the latest storm or circumstance with which you are confronted. Although people plan and stay consciously aware of the existence of laws they must obey, they sometimes try to challenge them. People drink alcohol and insist upon driving even though they know they have had too much to drink. Somehow, though, they believe that the law prohibiting drinking and driving does not apply to them personally. Thousands of needless deaths occur each year as a result. Therefore, our opinions about these principles will not change them. We all wish that working on ourselves and changing our expectations could be easy, but there is no magic wand or quick fix. You must begin the process of working on yourself to reset your expectations for life. Psychologists have said that eighty-seven percent of the average person's self-talk is negative, and that a person has 40,000 to 50,000 thoughts each day. This negative self-talk and negative expectancy results in eighty-seven percent of your magnetic ability coming from your outer self attracting things you do not want. So what if you begin to lower that eighty-seven percent more and more everyday and begin to raise the percentage of your positive self-talk, deliberately turning your magnet up to attract what you do want in life?

I talked with a pilot in TGI Friday's restaurant in the Pittsburgh airport while on a layover one day. I had always thought that the air moving underneath the wing of a plane lifts it into the air and keeps it up there. He explained to me, however, that that is not the way planes fly at all. The wing of a plane is constructed so that the air moving over the top of the wing moves faster than the air moving under the wing. The faster-moving air above the wing actually draws the plane up into the air. Therefore, the plane is lifted from the top of the wing rather than from the bottom of the wing. Planes fly overhead everyday because someone discovered how to lift objects and put this law into effect. There is a lower level consisting of facts, and one such fact is the existence of gravity. None of us will dispute the fact that gravity is real, but there are certain people who have found a higher level of facts consisting of superceding laws, principles, and benchmarks. When you begin to operate according to those superceding laws and principles, the facts on a lower level, which counted very much while you were operating on that lower level, cease to count. Why? Because you have found higher laws. You can pick something up right now and drop it onto the floor. Although the existence of gravity is real and affects you greatly on one level, when you put the law of lift and thrust into action then the effect of gravity is suspended. A plane will stay in the air as long as there is enough fuel to keep it up there.

Expanding your expectations is one way to move beyond the lower level of facts that stop most people. When your expectations are expanded, you are able to move beyond your supposed limitations to a higher level. As a result, you create a larger container in which to receive. For example, it would be ludicrous to collect water from the ocean with a thimble. Try to envision a man standing by the ocean holding a thimble. A person walks up to him and asks why he's holding it. He replies, "Well, I came here to get some water out of the ocean. Don't you know this is how you're supposed to get water out of the ocean? This is how my parents and their parents did it. And you know what? I saw a guy here a few weeks ago who brought buckets to the ocean to get water. Isn't that ridiculous? Even more ridiculous than that was a guy a couple of months ago who brought 55 gallon drums to get water out of the ocean. But the most ridiculous was someone years ago who came here with an oil tanker and filled the tanker with water. How presumptuous!"

45

Although that illustration may sound kind of funny, in reality, that's what many people do. They come to the ocean, which represents the dream or the higher level that is available to them. When they arrive to collect "water" with a container that is too small, then there's no way to receive the largeness of what they are very passionately desiring in life. **Expanding one's expectations enlarges the container, which then enlarges the capacity to receive.**

The Power of Expectations

So the first step is to verbalize your expectations. The next step is to write them down. What does this accomplish? First of all, as you speak the words out loud, something wonderful happens. The words go out of your mouth, unguarded, and into your ears and heart, reaffirming and strengthening purpose-based principles. Sharing expectations with other people is also very beneficial. Again, you must choose very carefully the people with whom you talk about your expectations. If you talk to the right people about your purpose and the wonderful dreams you have for your life, they will become a source of inspiration to you if they are also moving toward a higher level themselves. Although you unconsciously talk to yourself often, beginning to talk deliberately to yourself can seem a bit uncomfortable at first. But with time, talking to yourself will become very natural and even automatic. You must become your own cheerleader to keep your positive expectations wide open. One good reason to talk to yourself is because it might be the only positive conversation you have all day. By talking positively to yourself, writing down your expectations and reviewing what you have written each day, you align yourself with the five percent of people who achieve their dreams. Ninety-five percent of all people refuse to formalize their dreams, thinking that the process is crazy or will take too much discipline. The fact is, the more you practice this, the easier it gets and the more you start to wonder why anyone would want to live any other way.

The ability to expand one's expectations is also connected to a strong sense of worthiness. The knowledge that you are worthy and that you deserve to fulfill your dreams becomes crucial. If you do not feel worthy, one of two things will happen. One option is that you will never reach your next level and all the things that go along with it. The second option is that, even if by chance, you trip over the line and seem to receive some of the benefits you are searching for, you will not feel worthy and, as a result, will make sure that you sabotage yourself. You will lose these benefits because you do not feel you are worthy of them in the first place.

Find The Right Mirror

In contrast, **if you know you are worthy and deserving of your next level you become absolutely persistent.** You will not be denied and will not quit. When Thomas Edison endeavored to perfect any of his inventions, whether it was the light bulb or the battery, he would make as many as 10 to 50,000 attempts before he would actually make one of the inventions work. When he was asked once how he could keep his spirits up after trying so many times to invent something, he said he knew he had to succeed because he would eventually run out of ways that it would not work. Edison was an example of a person who believed he was worthy and that it was his destiny to reach that higher level. Expanding one's expectations is integrally connected to this sense of worthiness. You can continue to expand your expectations to the extent that you have a strong sense of deserving your dream. **This sense of worthiness is connected to the picture you have of yourself.** I remember going to Disneyland years ago. As I walked into the arcade, I saw a row of mirrors to one side. I looked in the first mirror and my head looked about six inches long and my legs looked about ten feet tall. I went to the next mirror and my head looked about ten feet long and my legs looked about six inches tall. In another mirror I looked extremely large, and in another, like a bean pole stretching to heaven. Each of those mirrors showed an extreme distortion of what I really looked like. But if I had never seen an accurate mirror, I probably would have believed that was how I really looked.

Throughout life you have a picture of yourself that has been created by your family or others who reared you. Sometimes this picture is good, and sometimes, unfortunately, it is distorted. Influences such as the media tell you how to look, dress, and act. You are also affected by successes and failures, and by your education (or lack of education).

The sum of these influences and how you feel you measure up to them creates the picture you have of yourself. You desperately need to return to an accurate picture. You see, you are not merely the outer self. When you look into the wrong mirror you only see your outer surface identity. You begin to evaluate your self-worth according to your accomplishments or outer conduct. And you feel, because you have failed or have made a mistake or have tried and tried without success, you are a failure. You neglect to realize, however, that your identity is not on the outside. That explains why people can stoop to the depths of despair and then rebound. They can go to the bottom of the barrel. They can break through the bottom and go even lower so that they have to look up to see the bottom and then decide that, with God's help, their life will be different in the future. They can begin to apply principles and begin to establish themselves with powerful benchmark laws. Then they can soar from the bottom to heights they barely imagined possible. Such people realize that the picture of their outer selves does not define them. They realize that who they are on the inside is their true image or identity. When this shift takes place, everything in life begins to change.

This change requires that you take a second look at all the things which have influenced your self-image. With an open mind and a fresh look with your inner eyes, you must consider the possibility that some of the things your parents told you, or that you were taught by society, were not totally accurate. Certainly the belief that if you go to college, then you will get a good job, work hard for thirty years, get a gold watch, retire, and then live happily ever after is not reality. Begin to ask the question *Who am I really?* If you look in the right "mirror," you will realize that you are an eternal being with unlimited possibilities. You will be able to tell yourself that you are indestructible, full of love, filled with ability, totally worthy, created to succeed, and born to soar. Once you realize that the real you is who you truly are, then you can look daily at the picture you have formed of yourself and make sure it matches who you are on the inside.

In the play "The Man of La Mancha," Don Quixote was riding down the road on his horse with his companion riding by his side. As they stopped to rest at a little cantina, Don Quixote and the gentleman riding with him dismounted from their horses and sat at a table while the attendant led the horses off for water and rest. A young lady came from the kitchen carrying two beverages and set them in front of the two men. Don Quixote looked up and said to her, "Oh my goodness! You are so beautiful and wonderful. You are my lady, Dulcinea." She looked at him, angrily, and said, "I am not Dulcinea. I am not beautiful or wonderful. You do not know me. I am Aldonza, I am nothing." And then she ran off. Later in the play this same thing happened again as Don Quixote and his companion traveled down the road. They saw someone lying off to the side of the road. Don Quixote dismounted his horse and walked over to the person, realizing it was the young lady. He declared, "Oh my, you are more beautiful than ever. You are wonderful and radiant. You are my lady, my Dulcinea." She jumped to her feet and looked at him with more anger, saying, "Why do you keep saying that? I am filthy and lower than dirt. I am a prostitute like my mother was. Don't you see the cuts and bruises on my face? Don't you see my ripped and tattered dress? I have just been raped by a gang of night travelers. Don't call me Dulcinea. I am Aldonza, I am worth nothing." And then she ran away.

In the last scene of the play, Don Quixote is lying in his bed on his estate. A young lady walks through the front gate and down a cobblestone walkway. She walks in the front door and back to the bedroom, where all of Don Quixote's family and friends have gathered around his bed. They know it is only a matter of minutes or hours before he will die. She walks over to his bed and puts her hand on his arm. He opens his eyes and tries to focus with all his strength. As he begins to see her more clearly, he says, "oh my goodness, you are beautiful. Your hair, the beautiful dress you are wearing, and the glow on your face are all wonderful. But even more beautiful is the love I feel coming from your eyes and the warmth I feel from your heart. Who are you? Do I know you? What is your name?" She then replies, "Yes, you know me. I am Dulcinea. I am the one you believed me to be."

In life, you will become the person you believe and picture yourself to be. The more you work on seeing the right picture of yourself, the stronger your sense of worthiness will become. And the stronger your sense of worthiness, the greater your ability to expand your expectations, using your magnetic ability to draw your dream-purpose toward you. This whole process begins with making a decision; starting at the benchmark of expanding your expectations. In doing so, you are literally predetermining what you are going to attract and receive in life.

There is a line in "The Man of LaMancha" that Don Quixote says when someone tries to talk him out of his dreams and visions of life. He says, "It is madness to settle for reality as it is rather than as it could be." **You can deliberately determine where you are going in life.** It really does not matter how many times you fall down in the process, or how many mistakes you make. **If your heart is right and you are going in the right direction and working the right principles, the number of times you fall is not important. The important thing is whether you keep getting up again.**

Stay on Course

Throughout the course of a several hour flight, a plane will wander off course many times, but through computerized instruments and the intervention of pilots, the plane is constantly being brought back on course so it will reach the right destination. In the same way, you must begin to say the right things to yourself **before you even get out of bed in the morning.** Begin to get in the habit of making reality check statements to yourself while you begin to wake up, such as *I am the offspring of the Creator. I am God's creation. I was born to succeed. I am worthy of my dream.* When you concentrate on such statements before you are even fully awake, you will become centered. By establishing this as a habit for the first few minutes of each day, you will circumvent the normal process of what happens, which is, as soon as your feet hit the floor, you are running around the outer perimeter of your life thinking about all the things you need to get done. Although you may already have a time set aside for prayer and reading in the morning, you will find that making these reality check statements will add to the power of any of your prayers or meditation.

As you continue getting ready for the day, talk to yourself some more, maybe when you are in the shower, or when you eat breakfast. Hang notes stating positive principles on the bathroom mirror, on the dashboard of your car, on your calendar, on the refrigerator, or in other places where you will see them continually. **You must make a deliberate effort to focus on an accurate positive picture of yourself in order to counteract the negative influences you will encounter throughout the day.** Some examples of statements you can say or write to yourself are: *I am an eternal being with unlimited possibilities. I was created for a great purpose. I have a great destiny. I will live this day filled with positive thoughts about myself I will flow from who I really am on the inside. Everything God created is good. I am filled with purpose, strength, creativity, versatility, and ability. When I have gone as far as I feel I can go, God will take me the rest of the way.* Constantly affirm the truth about yourself throughout the day no matter what other activity you are involved in. Keep the right picture of yourself and maintain a strong sense of worthiness, ensuring that your expectations for the day, as well as for the future, are expanded as wide and as large as possible.

As you keep yourself focused you will find that the other areas of your life will come into alignment and begin to prioritize themselves properly. These other areas include such things as work, health, family life, money, and involvement in activities such as church or other organizations. By keeping focused on who you really are on the inside, a cycle is created in which your "outer" life literally begins to facilitate the purpose and dream coming from within you.

In the first chapter of Psalms, there is a passage stating that as you meditate day and night on the law, you will be like a tree planted by rivers of water. And you will bring forth in your season, and your leaf will not wither, and whatever you do will prosper. Keeping yourself focused on the right principles is really what the psalmist is talking about in this chapter. Another benefit to keeping yourself focused is that it eliminates the need to try to fix other people in your life. When you are centered, you often very naturally become a catalyst for change in the lives of people around you without struggling to do so. You have heard the scripture which talks about knowing the truth will make you free. Well, that includes the truth about you! As you concentrate on the truth about who you were meant to be, then positive and constructive actions will be a natural automatic outcome. Everything you do will begin to facilitate your dream and your journey to the next level. No longer will your life simply consist of running around putting out fires in different areas of your life. The challenges of life will simply be what they are, and nothing more. They will facilitate movement to a higher level. When you consistently practice the right principles, you foster a greater sense of deservedness and expand your expectations, causing a breakthrough in your life and enabling you to accomplish more than you ever dreamed possible. Most of the world is doing it backwards. Most people around you try to change themselves from the outside in, but changing oneself truly is an inside job.

A Father's Lesson

When he was five years old, Hunter walked into his father's study and said, "Dad, come out and play." His dad said, "Hunter, I have to work. I have a lot of work that I brought home from the office and I have to get this stuff done tonight." "Yeah, but Dad, you're always working. Come out and play." His dad replied, "No Hunter, I have to finish this work. Please leave and shut the door when you go." Hunter came in a few minutes later and said, "Please Dad, come out and play." His father replied, "I'll tell you what. I'll come out and play when I'm all done." A frustrated Hunter left the office and slammed the door behind him. A third time, Hunter sheepishly entered the office and said, "Dad, when are you gonna be done? When can we play?" By then, Hunter's father realized his son was partially right; he really does work a lot and they had not had much time together lately. He reached into his office drawer and pulled out a magazine. He found a page with a picture of the world and ripped it out of the magazine. He ripped the paper into 16 pieces and gave the pieces to Hunter, along with a piece of cardboard and a bottle of glue. "Hunter," he said, "go to the kitchen table. You saw the picture of the world before I ripped it up. Take all of these pieces and put the world back together like in the picture. Pretend it's a puzzle and glue them on the cardboard. When you're done putting it back together, then I'll play ball with you." Hunter left the room and the father thought, *Great, I have at least 45 minutes. That will give me plenty of time to finish my work.* Five minutes later, Hunter strutted into the office with a smile on his face and said, "Dad, I'm all done." His father thought, *This is impossible. There is no way he could have put the world back together that quickly.* Looking at the piece of cardboard, he was absolutely amazed. There before him, although there were a few crooked pieces, every piece of paper was put together properly to form the world. Hunter's father asked, "Son, how did you do this? You don't know where all the countries of the world are." Hunter looked at his father and said, "It was very simple, Dad. As you were ripping up that page, I noticed there was a picture of a man dressed in a suit on the other side of the page. So it was easy. All I did was turn all the pieces of paper over and, when I got the man put together right, the world was right, too." We can learn a lot from little Hunter. His creative solution for solving the puzzle illustrates a point which is simple, yet easily forgotten. **When we "get right" by flowing from who we really are on the inside, our personal outer world will become right too.**

As I mentioned earlier in this book, I moved to Detroit when Les Brown and I began to work together. At that time things were very tight financially, and I had to practice a lot of delayed gratification on the way to my next higher level. Not only was I going through some financial difficulty, but so was Les. As a result, we moved out of the house we were living in and slept on the floor of Les' office in downtown Detroit. That was a time in life when we had to use every resource available to stay focused. Every night I would lie down on the office floor, pray, and meditate on principles for a while. I would listen to tapes of people who spoke on principles of truth that really nourished me at that point in my life. Many times I would drift off to sleep with a tape playing and the tape recorder would turn off by itself. As soon as I would wake up in the morning, I would, once again, pray and say positive things to myself. Then I would listen to the tape again for several minutes while waking up to let the encouraging words saturate my mind. After cleaning up for the day in the public restroom, I would come back to the office and read some of a book, listen to some more of a tape, and then begin the activity of the day. Without this daily program I would have lost focus, quit pursuing my purpose and given up on my dream. I will deal more with setting up your daily program in chapter five of this book.

I encourage you to follow a similar program every day of your life; not only in rough times, but also when things seem to be going great. Following a consistent program helps you develop and maintain a greater sense of worthiness and a clearer picture of who you truly are.

Chapter

4

Get In The Presence of Great People — Avoid Low-flying People

"Observing your close
friends will speak
volumes about you."
—*Unknown*

"Knowledge must come
through action."
—*Sophocles*

Outer Self - The Vehicle

Feeds on outside influences, perceptions and illusions

Energy drainer

THE REAL YOU — THE DRIVER

Nourished by purpose and principles

Power generator

Lives on truth-based reality

Lives by diversion and delusion

The state of your mind, will, and emotions is determined by the thoughts that you allow to dominate your consciousness and whether they are feeding the real you or the outer self

Get in the Presence of Great People — Avoid Low-Flying People

If you want to be great in any area of life, you must place yourself in the presence of people who are manifesting the level of greatness you desire. People tend to become like the people with whom they spend the most time. If you desire financial freedom, do whatever it takes to associate with people who have achieved a level of financial independence. If you want spiritual strength, associate with people who are spiritually strong. If you want to be a great mother to your children, spend time with someone you consider to be an excellent mother and learn from her example. You could spend many years at the finest university in the country studying to become a surgeon. Although such education is necessary and indispensable, time spent in the operating room with a master surgeon is just as crucial. Sometimes knowledge gained while in the presence of a great person is more valuable than what you learn on your own, and knowledge that is "caught" while in their presence can be just as valuable as that which is deliberately taught.

The distinction between the real you and your outer self becomes very clear when in the presence of a great person. A great person becomes great by focusing who they are on the inside to control his or her life. As a result, the qualities associated with flowing from the inside are evident in a great person's life. As you can see on the diagram, the real you generates power and is nourished by purpose and principles. The outer self, on the other hand, drains you of energy and feeds on outside influences, perceptions, and illusions; The real you lives according to truth-based reality. The outer self, however, feeds on superficial perceptions and illusions rather than anything solid. **The quality of your life is closely tied to whether you think positive or negative thoughts.**

Great People Have the Ideas

Great people value ideas, and they realize that **one idea can change everything.** As you spend time with a great person, his or her creativity will become contagious. I once heard of a salesman who acquired new leads by following his competitors' delivery trucks. He would then go to the same businesses and sell a product that was superior to his competitors' products. Watching the way creative people treasure and work with ideas can teach you valuable lessons.

Great People Have the Contacts and Connections

I have spent days worrying about how to solve a problem or how to make a situation in my business or personal life work. Often, all I needed to do was to discuss my dilemma with a great person who had already been down the same "road" and who could either give me advice or refer me to someone who could tell me how to solve my problem quickly and easily. Building a relationship with one great person will inevitably result in connections with a multitude of other great people. The saying, "Sometimes it's not what you know, but who you know, that matters," is truer today than ever before.

Great People Know Where the Land Mines Are and Where the Gold is Buried

While your own experience is often a great teacher, other peoples' experiences are often a better teacher. People who are operating on your desired level have already overcome certain obstacles and pitfalls on the way there. Why run into walls you could have avoided, or lose a leg to land mines that a great person could have warned you about ahead of time? Some people are determined to reinvent the wheel continually, but pride- and ego have a very costly price tag when you disregard the guidance of someone who has already been down the road on which you are traveling.

Besides knowing what to avoid, great people also know how to achieve success because they know where the gold is buried. Every person alive has the same 24 hours each day in which to accomplish things, yet some people use their time efficiently and achieve financial success. By spending time in the presence of successful people, you will learn that their income is the result of the service they provide and the problems they solve for other people. Helping other people make their dreams come true is part of their image and everyday activity. It does not matter whether you provide a cleaning product that removes spots from clothing, develop better parenting ideas, educate others about buying a house, or negotiate for world peace, **truly great people know that the more you give to others the more you will receive.**

Great People Know When to Talk and When to Be Silent

Another benefit of being in the presence of great people is having the opportunity to observe how carefully they choose their words.

61

Knowing when to talk and when to keep silent is very important. You have seen people who talk non-stop and eventually lose value in the eyes of those who are listening. Great people speak in a way that makes everyone comfortable and cognizant of their integrity. There is no substitute for being in their presence. As you encounter these people who are living dreams similar to your own, observe them and begin to do as they do. You will find that you will get closer to becoming the same kind of person.

Make Great Associations

To a great extent, success in life is the result of great associations. You will learn many valuable lessons in the presence of extraordinary people. You may be wondering, *How do I place myself in the presence of these great people who are already living on a higher level ?* A few times in my life I have taken great measures to get in the presence of a great person. Each time that association resulted in my life taking a quantum leap to the next level. At times, I had to lay my foolish ego aside to get in a person's presence. I would spend money traveling to see such a person without thinking twice. But I never just followed a whim. Each time I recognized a definite connection and reason for me to be in the presence of a particular person.

When I was only twenty years old, I sat in a crowd of over 60,000 people listening to a man from Canada named Brian Ruud speak. Never in my life had I heard anyone speak with such absolute belief and deliver a message that completely revolutionized my life. As I watched him speak, I thought to myself, *I'm going to speak like him someday and share important principles.* A week later, I found out he was to speak in Minneapolis, Minnesota. So I flew to Minneapolis, found the auditorium where he was speaking, and listened to his entire talk. After the meeting, Brian went back to his tape and book table to sign autographs. I waited off to the side until the crowd was gone and almost everyone had gone home. As Brian was about to leave, I walked up to him and said, "Hi Brian. I'm Larry DiAngi. Is there anything I can do to help you?" "Yes," Brian replied, "you could give my staff a hand moving boxes." After helping load the boxes onto a truck, I was invited by Brian's employees to join them for dinner and ended up sitting next to Brian at the table. While we were eating, I finally mustered up the courage to ask Brian the question I had traveled all that way to find an answer to. "Brian, how can I become a speaker like you and do what you are doing? I believe that is what I'm supposed to do with my life." He turned to me and asked, "Larry, what are you doing right now as a full-time occupation?" I explained that I played drums in rock bands on weekends and worked in a shop during the week. He said, "Well, the best way for you to learn how to do what I am doing is to go back home and talk to the principals of all the high schools in your hometown, asking them to let me speak in their schools. Once you have booked me to speak in the schools, you will need to secure a building where I can hold an open rally each evening for seven nights. During the high school assemblies I will encourage the students to come to the evening rallies and bring their parents with them."

I agreed to do what Brian had asked and when I got home, I made an appointment with every principal at every high school in the city. I called Brian and said, "It's all set. I booked eight high schools and have a place for you to speak seven nights straight." There was a silence over the phone, and then Brian spoke, saying, "Larry, I never thought you could do it. In fact, I wasn't sure I would ever hear from you again."

Brian came to town and spoke to every high school in the city during the day, and we averaged between 600 and 800 people each night at the rallies. I chauffeured him around town, got him coffee, ran errands, secured people to help sell books and tapes, set up hotel and restaurant reservations, and did many other things. Though I received much inspiration and learned a lot working with Brian I never asked to be paid a penny. Someone once said, "Successful people are those who are willing to do many things that unsuccessful people feel they are too good to do." You may wonder why I would expend that kind of time and energy to be a "gopher" who does not even get paid. I did it for several reasons. First, I knew there was a connection, a reason I needed to be in Brian's presence. I wanted to try and figure out the secrets to his success. Second, I believed in Brian's message. Third, I had accepted the principle that; **the price for success must be paid in advance.** Forth, we became like brothers and even though there was work involved, it didn't seem like work because we were having such a great time. After helping Brian set up meetings for a few months, I finally secured my first out-of-town speaking engagement. I have been traveling and speaking to groups ever since. I don't believe it was simply by chance that I was sitting in that audience the first time I heard Brian speak. Many times I have thanked God for allowing me to be at the right place at the right time. After 20 years I can still see the affect that knowing Brian has had on my life.

Five years after meeting Brian Ruud, I met another extraordinary person named David Minor, Sr. A great minister, Reverend Minor influenced my life and helped me move to the higher level I was working toward at that time. As I observed David Minor and spent time in his presence, I realized he was well-respected and honored by thousands of people across the United States. He continually displayed a sincere humility and compassion which seemed to be the driving force in his life and resulted in him being a blessing to countless people across the United States. Nine years later I met Les Brown.

Each time I attempted to get in the presence of a great person, I tried to be valuable and of service in some way. I learned that the way to gain the respect of great people is not to act superior in their presence, but to demonstrate a willingness to serve. Extraordinary people know that **the greatest among us will be those who have learned to serve the best.** This principle applies in the business world as well as in every other area of life. If you want to figure out a way to place yourself in the presence of great people, find a way to be of service to them. Get them a cup of coffee, open the car door for them, or invite them to dinner. Take them to a very nice restaurant and pull out all the stops. The amount you spend on dinner will be miniscule compared to the priceless influence such a person will have on your life.

Your own observations while in the presence of a great person will be extremely valuable. The opportunity to watch a great person walk into a room, handle conversations, or deal with objections and sticky situations can often be the best teacher. If you ever get the chance to sit quietly, like a mouse, and listen to such a person conduct business on the phone for an entire day, take it. You will receive more of an education than if you spent months in a classroom learning negotiating skills. A multimillionaire once said if he lost every penny he had made, he would save enough money to buy a fine suit, go into the finest restaurant in town, and just sit and drink coffee. He would listen to all the successful people, soaking up enough ideas to go back out and make his fortune all over again. **Great people demonstrate over and over again that their motivation comes from within.** When you are living in a way that is compatible with the real you, then the circumstances of your life do not matter. What you do about the circumstances matters. You have the power to turn the negative in your life to positive.

Avoid the "Low Flyers" in Life

While getting in the presence of great people is crucial, it is just as important to avoid the "low flyers" in life. These are people whose aspiration in life is to fly just high enough to avoid hitting the curb. They have no concept of the heavens, or that soaring through them is even a possibility. Some of your family members may even be like this. It is possible to love someone but refuse to let them steal your dreams or pull you down to a lower level. You can love these people, but you do not have to spend much time around them. I have found that there are "thirty minute" people in life. After thirty minutes in their presence, I know it is time for me to leave. I have found "fifteen minute" people as well, and even a few "one second" people. When I encounter them, I just wave and say "Hi" and keep walking. Why? Because I have learned that spending more than a second in their presence is toxic and requires that I build myself back up afterwards. Being in their presence causes me to drift toward the outer part of myself where negativity resides.

There was a man named John who lived back in the "horse and buggy" days before sidewalks were common. One day he was walking down a narrow path through a field with thick, thorny bushes on both sides of the path. Looking down while he walked, he suddenly raised his eyes to realize that his most ardent enemy was walking towards him. Finally they met toe to toe, nose to nose, and eye to eye. His enemy looked him in the eye and said, "John, I never step out of the way for a fool." John thought for a second then courteously stepped aside and said, "I always do, please you go first." Now, I would not recommend that exact approach. But when someone is shooting negative arrows with their words at us, on the inside we can step aside and let them fly by.

Some people refuse to go to their higher level and it becomes their mission in life to keep everyone else down with them. I have a saying that I use in many of my talks, which is: "You should never listen to a person telling you that you cannot go to a place they have never been before." Such people will look you in the eye and say you are crazy to think you can live your dream. They will try to make you doubt your creativity and ability. You need to look at them and say these words to yourself: *I love you, but you just don't understand. I have a dream-purpose. I will not let you hold me down.* Many times they are just trying to help you avoid disappointment by reminding you not to get your hopes up. But you must remember that they are not basing that advice on anything reliable. In fact, their advice is worth exactly what you pay for it, which is nothing. I do not want to be too hard on these people, only to stress that you need to protect yourself from being around dream stealers who will inhibit your personal growth. Let their attitudes, words, and actions fly by without piercing you.

Great People Challenge You To Be Your Best

As you avoid the "low flyers" in life, you must also be careful not to surround yourself with people who agree with whatever you say. When you begin to accomplish greater things in life, it is easy to surround yourself with people who give you their stamp of approval no matter what you say or do. Although we all like to be stroked and told that we are a great person, surrounding yourself with such people will not help you get to your next level. Instead, you need to **find people who will make you stretch and grow continually, and who are not afraid to tell you when you are wrong.** They can challenge you to get back on track with principle-based advice when you are not operating from the real you. What I am really talking about here is surrounding yourself with people who **love you more than they like you.**

When Les Brown and I first started working together years ago, I observed that he would never quit working at five or six o'clock. Often, we would be up until two o'clock in the morning working on our dream. At one point I needed $2000 within two days to pay for overdue bills. The creditors were calling me and were about to get "very serious." To make matters worse, my car had been stolen in Detroit two weeks prior to that time. Down in the dumps, I walked into Les' office at one o'clock one morning and said, "Les, we're sleeping here in the office, my car's been stolen, and I need $2000 dollars in two days or I'm in big trouble."

Les looked at me and said, "You know Larry, I've been thinking about a lot of the same things. As you know, I'm facing some pretty serious financial challenges myself right now. But for some reason the thought keeps going through my mind that if money can solve our problem, then we really don't have a problem." Those words changed my thinking completely. We could always find a way to make more money. The next day I got up early, got on the phone, and made over a hundred phone calls. I finally found someone in Texas who would pay me $3000 to speak three times in one day. They also agreed to overnight me a check for $2000, exactly the amount I needed, as a deposit to secure that date on my calendar. What was it that got me up that day and motivated me to turn a potential tragedy into victory? It was being in the presence of a great person.

Chapter

5

Feed Your Power Source Constantly

"What this power is I cannot say, all I know is that it exists and it becomes available only when a man is in that state of mind in which he knows exactly what he wants and is fully determined not to quit until he finds it."
—*Alexander Graham Bell*

"The biggest lesson I have ever learned is the stupendous importance of what we think. If I knew what you think, I would know what you are, for your thoughts make you what you are By changing our thoughts, we can change our lives."
—*Dale Carnegie*

The Outer Self

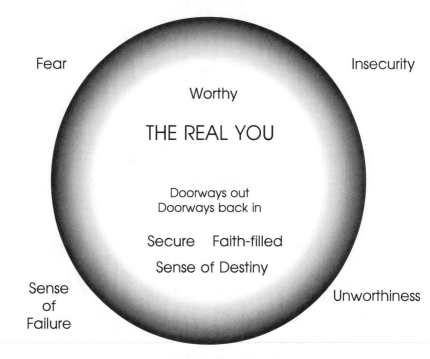

Frustration

Fear

Insecurity

Worthy

THE REAL YOU

Doorways out
Doorways back in

Secure   Faith-filled

Sense of Destiny

Sense
of
Failure

Unworthiness

You were not born with feelings of insecurity, unworthiness, failure, fear, frustration, etc. As you grow older, you travel progressively away from the real you through doorways of negative experiences which cause you to feel vulnerable or manipulated.

As you begin now from the real you, you encounter similar experiences again, but this time you respond from the secure and faith-filled part of you. Each time you face these similar experiences and become victorious, that "victory" allows you to go back through that doorway into the real you.

Feed Your Power Source Constantly

The longer you deprive any living thing of nourishment, the weaker it will become. All of nature affirms this principle. If you deprive your physical body of food, you will experience weakness very quickly. The real you is no exception. When you starve your inner being, you become weaker and weaker inside. Every moment you are either feeding your real, inner being, or your outer imposter self. When you feed one and starve the other, the one that is nourished and fed will gain control.

Most people have a very strong outer self. They have fed this aspect of themselves with the media, opinions they have developed in life, and things their parents told them and convinced them were facts about life. Many of the ideas that govern your life were formed at a very early age. Some of these ideas you accepted as reality simply because you were reared in an environment in which they made perfect sense. One such idea, which is really a myth, is that you can create security through a job with "good benefits." But in reality, there is no security in jobs or possessions. Real security exists only within yourself. The more you feed the real you, the stronger you will become. Many of the inaccuracies cast upon you in life will be exposed. As you steadily feed your power source, all of the dysfunction that exists in the outer self begins to lose its grip and its power over you.

Throughout this book, I have talked about two places you can operate from. The real you, which is indestructible and full of peace, and the outer self, which is insecure and fearful. As you can see in the

71

diagram, doorways can be created which lead out to the outer self and back inside again. You were born operating from the real you. You innately knew security, worthiness, fearlessness, and peace. Babies do not worry about anything and when they get hungry or need a diaper changed they do not struggle with feelings of unworthiness, they simply open their mouth and use the only language they know and cry until they attract food or a fresh diaper. But as you grew (and continue to grow) older, you traveled into the outer self through doorways of negative experiences which caused you to feel vulnerable, insecure, or manipulated and, as a result, pulled you farther away from who you really are. These negative experiences may even have been with family members or friends who were not supportive of your purpose. But you do not have to allow your outer self to reign, causing you to feel inadequate or stagnant. You can allow the real you to take control.

Now let's look at what determines which part of you is in control of your life. Control begins with one thing, and that is a thought. If you plant a thought, you reap an act. If you plant an act, you reap a habit. If you plant a habit, you reap your lifestyle. If you plant your lifestyle, you reap your destiny. But it all starts with one thought, and **the collection of your thoughts becomes your philosophy in life. Your philosophy in life becomes your reality. Your reality creates your life.** Thoughts determine every aspect of your life. Thoughts affect your spiritual life, because only the real you is spirit.

Thoughts also affect your interaction with others, determining the quality and texture of your relationships. There is a drastic difference between two peoples' outer selves connecting and two peoples' true, inner person connecting.

Your financial life is affected by your thoughts, also, in that money can give either the outer self or the real you fuller expression. In fact, money just gives people the power to express who they truly are more fully. Money gives a person who is mean or controlling greater power and leverage to be even meaner and more controlling. If a person is truly benevolent, then money will provide greater leverage to express that as well. When your outer self is in control, you live in continual stress because, in your heart, you know you are not maintaining personal integrity. You are fighting a losing battle when you try to make life work solely on the strength of your outer self. The good news, though, is that no matter how far you travel south, when you turn around, you're automatically going north again. No matter how far you travel to the furthest regions of your outer self, you can always turn around and go back home to the real you.

The Power Of Thoughts

Your thoughts determine whether you are maintaining an inward or an outward focus on a day to day, hour to hour, minute to minute, and second to second basis. You see, even though we know that we are really only one person on the inside, we can seem like many different people on the outside. Some people seem like one person before they have their coffee in the morning and a totally different person after they have had some caffeine. Imagine that you are having one of the worst days of your life. Everything is going wrong at work, you have received several calls from your child's school informing you that your child is causing problems, then you begin driving home from work and the muffler falls off, you drive over the muffler and your tire goes flat; you look in your trunk to find that there is no spare tire; you call a tow truck to tow your car to a garage which costs you $45.00; a taxi ride home costs you another $25.00; you walk in the front door, throw your coat over the back of a chair, kick your shoes off, sit down and say to yourself, "I just want to go to bed and forget that this day ever happened." Suddenly, there is a knock at your front door and you think, "Oh no, on a day like today, I don't even want to know who that is, I don't want to talk to anyone," but you open the door anyway. To your surprise it's Ed McMahon — TV cameras are rolling and Ed hands you a check and says, "you've just won $14,000,000!" In less than sixty seconds you change from being discouraged to feeling like the possibilities for your life are unlimited. You immediately begin to believe that big dreams can become a reality. I have some great news for you, you can become a person filled with unshakable belief in your dreams without winning the $14,000,000. You just need to continually focus on the right thoughts.

If the collection of thoughts you have embraced as the truth fosters a philosophy that you will never succeed spiritually, mentally, emotionally, in relationships, or financially, then your philosophy will manifest itself as reality in your life. But there is good news, and that is whatever your thoughts have created up to this point in your life, your thoughts can recreate anew. By changing your thoughts, you can change every area of your life.

The more you discipline yourself to live according to the right principles, the more the real you will be in control and the more you will prosper. Take time right now to picture what the highest and best would be for you in every facet of your life. No matter what you feel about this picture, the truth is that the real you deserves the best in every one of these areas. You must reject feelings of guilt or unworthiness when envisioning the best for yourself. The presence of negative feelings indicates that you need to change the thoughts that have allowed your outer self to gain control.

Establish A Daily Program

The quality of your life is directly related to the quality of your thoughts. Therefore, it is essential to have a daily program to keep your thoughts on track. If you believe it is difficult to make money, then that will be your reality. If you believe that by providing a great service or product and helping people live a purpose-driven life you will attract money in great abundance, then that will be your experience. If you believe that a relationship is a constant struggle between egos, then that will be your reality. But if you believe it is possible for the real you to have a relationship with another centered person, then that will be your reality. Whatever you truly expect is what you will experience. Remember the principle, "As he thinketh in his heart, so is he."

To keep your thoughts congruent with who you really are and with principles of success, you must continually work to counteract negative thoughts. Reading this book is strengthening the real you. It is vitally important to fill your days reading the right books, listening to principle-based teaching cassettes, inspirational music, and interacting with supportive people who are working on themselves in the same way.

The work you do on yourself is the most important work you will do in life. The rest of your world falls in place when you are centered. Your daily affirmation program will help center you, and you will get something new out of it each day. A line from a book or a paragraph will jump out at you and help you maintain focus one day, yet have no effect the next day. One day it might be listening to a tape of someone talking about principles, and another day music may be the thing that inspires you that day. For that reason, it is important to stick to your program every day — you never know which part of your program will be the exact thing you need to stay centered.

I cannot stress enough the power of your thoughts and the impact they can have in your life. In Romans 12:2 the scriptures tell us that we are transformed by the renewing of our mind. When you change your thoughts, you renew and reprogram your mind, which in turn changes your philosophy. **Your philosophy is not only what you think about, but also what your opinions are about what you think about.** Here's a story that illustrates the difference. There are two men on opposite ends of a county. One is on a golf course and the other is a farmer out in his fields. It is raining, and both men are experiencing the same downfall. The man playing golf is frustrated and cursing the rain because he has to stop playing golf. The farmer, however, is raising his hands towards heaven, thanking God for the rain that will save his crops. Although both men are thinking about the rain, their opinions about the rain are very different. One man was experiencing bliss while the other was in agony.

Reprogram Your Thoughts

How do you reprogram your thoughts, thereby changing your reality? You do it by maintaining a constant flow of inspiration into your ears and eyes, from the moment you wake up to the moment you fall asleep at night. Also choose carefully the words that come out of your mouth. We have all heard of time released cold medicine or time released Vitamin C. To stay centered, on purpose, and flowing from the Real You, you need a **daily program of time released inspiration, information, and influence** in your life. This consists of ten minutes here and there through out the day, assimilating empowering principles. (These ten minute doses are in addition to the more extended periods of time you invest in the morning, evening, or at other points during your daily schedule.) How many ten minute doses do we need each day? Each day is different. One day you may need three ten minute doses and another day you may need six. When ever you feel yourself slipping into the outer self with stress, fear, insecurity, etc., find ten or more minutes to recieve some inspiration or information from a book, tape, music, or influence from a purpose-driven friend, either in person or by talking with them on the phone. As I mentioned in Chapter 3, it is a great idea to get a jump on your day by affirming reality check statements before you get out of bed in the morning and are fully awake. After repeating principle-based statements, spend a few moments in prayer or meditation and read some book that inspires you spiritually. In addition to that reading, spend 10-15 minutes reading a book based on sound principles for living. While many of these types of books exist, make sure you choose ones that are relevant to your own life. Also, take time in the morning to listen to an inspirational tape. Do this while you're getting dressed, driving your car, making breakfast, or during the time you would otherwise spend absorbing negative news of the day on television. Although I believe keeping up with current events is important, morning is not the time to do it. Your mind is much more susceptible and impressionable in the morning, and you need that time to get yourself on the right track before doing anything else.

Throughout the day, have short amounts of time set aside to spend reading, listening to a motivational tape or music, or speaking with another purpose-driven person. Even a three minute phone conversation with a centered person will help. One day he may need a boost, the next day you may need one, while another day you may both be centered and the conversation will be like throwing a match on gasoline.

As you go to bed at night, go over in your mind the positive thoughts you have absorbed throughout the day. You may believe you do not have time to incorporate these habits, but the fact is, you cannot afford not to keep your thoughts right. Your self-development library of books, tapes, and music should be worth at least as much as your wardrobe. After all, which is more important — what's on the inside or outside?

One Friday afternoon, three different people asked what was wrong with me, commenting that my energy seemed low. I finally realized that I had gradually stopped reading books, listening to tapes, praying and meditating, and repeating positive thoughts to myself. I had slipped back into the routine of living to get "stuff" done. I had started living in the outer self again. That Friday afternoon, I left the office, went home, and spent the entire weekend reading books, listening to tapes, and talking to inspiring friends on the phone. When I opened my apartment door Monday morning to go back to the office, a different Larry walked out. I was centered and focused. I had spent all weekend feeding my power source, and that made a world of difference in my life.

I have a friend who had triple by-pass open heart surgery. He told me that he had become so accustomed to the presence of angina pain over a period of time that he didn't realize how much pain he had been living with until he recovered from the surgery and the pain was gone. Before the surgery he would say "I just have a little indigestion" and would excuse the pain away, pretending everything was OK. I heard a story about a hound dog laying on a front porch moaning and groaning. When a person passing by asked the owner of the dog, "Why is your dog moaning and groaning" the owner replied "Because he's laying on a nail". To that the passer by responded, "Than why doesn't he just get up and move to another spot?". The owner explained "Oh, he's not hurting bad enough to move, he's just hurting bad enough to moan and groan'!! Some people just lay around moaning and groaning and others decide to take action to change their thoughts, philosophy, and reality; therefore taking every area of their life to a higher level.

On the following page you will find an exercise that will help you locate the specific areas of your life you need to target and work on to become centered. To complete this exercise begin with column #1 "Areas of life." The first item is "Where I live." As you think about the house or apartment you live in, the carpet, lighting, the neighborhood, etc. on impulse and without rationalizing, write in column #2 the one word (from the eight words provided at the top of column #2) that best describes your immediate feelings about that area of your life. For this exercise to be effective you must be completely honest with yourself. You can live for years being frustrated in a specific area of your life and make excuses why it will never change. The purpose of this exercise is to identify the areas in which you are operating from your outer self. Write down in column #2 the first word that "hits" you the strongest when you think of where you live, who you live with, your vocation, etc. If you feel freedom, frustration, peace, fear, etc. then write that one word down. After you have completed column #2 you will immediately see the areas in which you need to change your thoughts and work on the most. Any areas with the words fear, frustration, hate, or restriction next to them are areas in which your outer self may be in control. Column #3 should not be filled in so quickly. Put some thought into what the first step would be to center yourself. It could be that you need to take a book out of the library to gain more knowledge, ask forgiveness of a friend or family member, or start looking for a new place to live. As you consider other areas of your life which are not listed in this exercise, you can use these same eight words from column #2 to discern whether you are flowing from the real you or operating from the outer self.

AREAS OF LIFE	PEACE - FEAR FREEDOM - RESTRICTION LOVE - HATE HOPE - FRUSTRATION	FIRST STEP TO GET IN FLOW AND BE WHO I AM
WHERE I LIVE		
WHO I LIVE WITH		
MY VOCATION OR HOW I ATTRACT MONEY		
THE CREATIVITY WHICH I POSSESS		
MARRIAGE - SPOUSE OR SIG- NIFIANCT OTHER		
MY PARENTS		
MY CHILDREN		
CLOSE FRIENDS		
MY PHYSICAL BODY		
MY MENTAL STATE		
MY SPIRITUALITY		
MY EMOTIONAL STATE		

Chapter

6

Do Things You've Never Done

"You must do the things today that others will not do so that you can have the things tomorrow that others will not have."
—*Unknown*

"Far better it is to dare mighty things, to win glorious triumphs, even though checkered by failure, than to rank with those poor spirits who neither enjoy much nor suffer much, because they live in the gray twilight that knows not victory nor defeat."
—*Theodore Roosevelt*

Outer Eyes

See only
the superficial

Obstacles
look
overwhelming

See problems
but not
solutions

INNER EYES

Inner eyes see with purpose
Possibilites unlimited
Clear vision
Creative
See Beyond Surface Circumstances
Self-acceptance

Blurred
perception

Dreams are
a
fantasy

Fearful

Your inner eyes see unlimited possibilites
because they allow creativity to flourish.
Your outer eyes see through a filter of negative
thoughts and experiences creating distorted vision.
Your inner eyes see life, situations, and people
clearly, as they really are.

Do Things You've Never Done

You were born with a built-in desire to create. Human beings are naturally more fulfilled when they can use their creative abilities, bringing something into existence which was not there before. By focusing your creativity, you can produce a greater flow of personal fulfillment into your life. You can also create a flow of great relationships, spiritual strength, business success, happiness in your marriage, and financial prosperity. But in order to create anything new in your life, you must personally experience growth. You must make a conscious effort to become who you are inside and cultivate your dreams.

When people refuse to grow, they are sentenced to live and operate from the outer self. Personal growth always involves stretching and pushing beyond the preconceived limitations you have set for yourself. As you continue to expand your expectations, place yourself in the presence of great people, and feed the "real" you continuously, you automatically become more of who you really are inside. As you let the real you gain control, you will have to begin doing some things you have never done. You will have to break out of your comfort zone and begin to create. To do this, you must overcome your fear of breaking out of the box that the outer self has kept you in for so long. You have to be willing to take some risks. Risking involves going beyond the way you normally do things so you can start being who you really are. As you flow from the real you, your actions will be an outgrowth of who you are inside. This involves moving away from a lower level to get to a higher level, and that can be scary. In my life, every time I reach for a higher level, it is always just far enough away that I have to let go of where I am to get there. Fear can only live in the outer self.

I am continually on planes flying from one speaking engagement to the next, and it is always amazing to watch planes take off and land at major airports. One plane lifts off the ground and, before it is even out of sight, another plane takes off right behind it. How is it possible for thousands of planes to take off and land each day? The main reason is because there is someone in the control tower coordinating all of the activity. You can view the real you and your outer self the same way. The outer self was not wired, nor does it have the ability, to keep all the different areas of your life in order and flowing properly. All of the different facets of our lives are like planes taking off and landing. **Only the real you can coordinate relationships, finances, spirituality, children, and all of the other areas of your life at the same time.** It is no wonder that areas of our lives crash and burn if nobody is in the control tower.

See Life Through Different Eyes

Another way of viewing the real you and your outer self is as inner and outer eyes, as illustrated in the diagram. To do things you have never done, you must begin to look at the mountains you will climb in life with different eyes. You have two sets of eyes. One set sees from your outer self, and the other sees from the real you. If the real you is in control, then you will see life with your inner eyes. If your outer self is in control, then you will see with your outer eyes. Your inner eyes see the purpose in your life and never lose sight of it. With clear vision, they see that the circumstances, or facts, of your life are small when compared to your dreams. The possibilities are unlimited and problems can be overcome.

In contrast, your outer eyes cannot see very far away, and what they do see is blurry. Your dreams are barely visible to your outer eyes because they get bogged down in the circumstances of life that challenge your purpose. They cannot see past the outer facts to the possibility that your dream could come true; they only see the problems that threaten your dream.

People become successful, to a great extent, because they see things differently than other people. There are people who have achieved financial freedom by building businesses around the world. They have marriages which have grown stronger over a period of decades and children who have successful careers. To a great extent, everything these families have accomplished and enjoy is the result of an inner vision.

A man who has demonstrated this principle in his own life like few others in history and has also helped thousands of other people to live their dreams is Dexter Yager, who says, "If the dream is big enough, the facts don't count." If you look at your dream with your outer set of eyes, the dream will never be big enough because outer vision is short-sighted. The dream looks smaller when compared with the challenges you must face. On the outside, your dream remains only a fantasy. When you give the real you the control, however, your dream becomes your purpose. It is no longer optional. Your reasons for wanting your dream become so important to you that the lower level facts or obstacles will not stop you. Remember this when you start to doubt your dream or your purpose. To the outer self, the realities of life look overwhelming. To the real you, the challenges or obstacles of life are simply stepping stones to your higher level. A powerful illustration of this principle is that you would normally not want to run out into a street in the path of an oncoming truck. Imagine this. What if you are at a friend's house sitting on the front porch visiting; your six-year-old child and their seven-year-old are playing with a ball in the front yard. All of a sudden the ball rolls out into the street and your child runs to get it. You look up the street to your left and see a truck speeding toward your child at what you would estimate to be 50 mph. You jump over the railing of the porch and your feet hit the ground running. You dash into the middle of the street, scoop up your child and leap with all your might to the other side of the street. As your feet leave the ground they scrape alongside the door of the truck. Then you find yourself rolling on the grass hugging your child repeating the words "Thank you God, thank you God." I have a question for you. What could have stopped you from running into the middle of that street? *Nothing.* You were looking at the challenge not with the outer eyes that say, "I *wonder if it will be worth it? Maybe I won't get there in time anyway."* or *"It's too much of a risk."* **You saw that situation from your inner eyes which see with 100% purpose. That's called, BEING PURPOSE DRIVEN.**

Success in life depends on how you view the opportunities and challenges which are presented to you. When looking at something with your outer eyes, you are able to see superficial characteristics such as color and shape. But when you look at the same object or situation with your inner eyes, you are able to see things you could not see with your outer eyes, such as how you can do something to change your life. When you see with your inner eyes, you recognize an opportunity in front of you instead of passing it by without noticing it is a vehicle to take you where you want to go.

I once heard a story illustrating how a person's inner vision helped her discover the price she had to pay to make her dream a reality. On the way to achieving financial freedom and living the dream life she and her family live now, she came to a point where she needed to reach a certain goal to reach her higher level. Although she loved boating, she decided not to go out on her boat until she reached her goal. She would use the time usually spent boating to work on mak-

ing her dream a reality. Although other people saw this decision as a great sacrifice, she did not see it as a sacrifice at all. She looked at her delayed gratification as a great investment. Instead of boating on the same old lake she had for years, she would be able to go boating in Hawaii or anywhere else she desired once she reached her goal.

As the story illustrates, reaching your goals involves practicing delayed gratification. You have two different ways of viewing what you have to give up to reach your higher level. When the facts seem too big and the sacrifice seems too great in comparison to your dream, then you need to work on your thoughts to create a different philosophy which will enable you to begin seeing with your inner eyes. Fear can hinder you from reaching your goals, and fear comes in many forms. Some of these forms include fear of making mistakes, fear of failure, fear of success, and fear of the unknown.

Make Making Mistakes OK

Making mistakes can show you how to do something better the next time and open up new possibilities. Have you ever been on your way somewhere and then ended up somewhere better because you took a wrong turn?

Fear of the Unknown

The unknown can be scary, but once you face it head-on, you realize the shadow is usually much larger than the actual obstacle or threat. The unknown can be like a mouse with a microphone — it sounds intimidating, but when you actually see the source of the noise, you realize it's not threatening at all.

Years ago I met a great person named Tony who has been instrumental in helping thousands of people find greater purpose and meaning in life. A story from his childhood shows how he overcame a haunting fear that threatened to affect every day of his life. One night as we were eating a wonderful Italian meal his mother had cooked, he told this story. As a child, Tony would walk the same route home from school every day. One day, new neighbors moved into a house down the street from his house. Tony immediately became aware of the fact that they owned a bulldog. When he got to the corner and crossed the street, the bulldog would dart out of the neighbors' backyard and chase him half a block to his house. Five days a week he would run with all his might and shut the gate to the fence in his front yard just before the dog could catch him. This went on for six months. One day, when he was in the restroom at school, Tony looked in the mirror and said to himself, *Tony, you're not going to run from that bulldog one more day.* That afternoon, he kept talking to himself as he walked home saying, *That bulldog may be bad, but he's not as bad as me.* Finally, still talking to himself, Tony got to that last corner and crossed the street. Just then, like clockwork, the bulldog started coming at him. Without thinking, Tony started running like he usually did. After a few steps, he thought to himself, *If I run from this dog one more day I may have to run the rest of my life.* Tony stopped dead in his tracks and decided he would do whatever it took to stop that dog. He reached down to grab the first thing he could find and picked up a brick. He swung around to face the barking bulldog. As Tony looked closely, he couldn't believe his eyes. There was not a single tooth in that bulldog's mouth. For six months, he had been running from a toothless bulldog! Tony proceeded to chase the bulldog back to the corner and the dog never bothered him again.

Don't Let others Discourage You

Every circumstance that tells you that you cannot live your dream is like that toothless bulldog. Every person who tries to talk you into settling for less than you deserve is like that toothless bulldog. Never let anyone tell you that you cannot go where they have never been. People will say "you can't do that" or "you can't go there," but when you ask them if they have ever done that or gone there, they will say no. The fact that they have never experienced what they are warning you against totally disqualifies them from giving you advice. It is amazing to listen to a person with no money tell someone else they will never make it in business and become financially independent. These "toothless bulldogs" are everywhere. But you will soon realize that if others cannot see and appreciate your dream, then they are looking out of the wrong pair of "eyes."

One way to stop running from your fears is to begin to observe yourself. Let's use the fear of talking to people to whom you feel inferior as an example. Think of someone you feel insecure around. When you look closely at what is happening, you see that you feel insecure because this person seems smarter, richer, better looking, or more powerful than you seem to yourself. But the truth is that everyone in the world is created equally. We may honor someone for the great things he has accomplished, but he is still no better than anyone else. We are all the offspring of God the Creator.

Suppose you are presenting a business proposal to someone. You know it is a wonderful opportunity and that he will profit greatly by accepting your proposal. But as you stand there talking, you feel inferior to him. Do not wait until ten minutes after the conversation is over and kick yourself as you think, *If only I would have said this or if only I had thought to say that.* Instead, while you are talking, observe yourself with your inner eyes. If you are experiencing insecurity or fear, then you know you are operating from the outer self because that is the only place fear and insecurity can live. Observing yourself in the moment enables you to center yourself. As you read this book, put your hand over your chest and say these words to yourself: I *live in here.* Observing yourself allows you to look inward and refocus, so you can view the same situation with your inner eyes. When the real you looks at the same situation, it will look totally different. You will realize, *Wait a minute. I don't need to feel insecure talking to this person. He got dressed just like me. He is a real person on the inside just like me. He wants love, acceptance, freedom, and the approval of others just like me.* Without fail, you will see things very differently when you look at life with your inner eyes. When you experience any negative emotion such as fear, doubt, insecurity, or guilt, handle them all the same way. Observe yourself from the inside out and refocus. You will begin to see the truth about your real identity.

We all make mistakes when we do things we have never done before. When you trip and skin your knee, remember that **only a worm cannot fall down. And when you do fall, make sure you fall forward, because then you will be between five and six feet closer to your dream.** Be the creator you were born to be. Create success, loving relationships, and fulfillment. As you become the great person you were born to be, you will find you can do some amazing things you never before dreamed possible.

Chapter

7

Hold The Vision — Know You Were Born To Soar

"Cherish your visions and
your dreams as they
are the children of your
soul; the blueprints of your
ultimate achievements."
—*Napoleon Hill*

"What lies behind us and what lies
before us are small matters
compared to what lies within us."
Ralph Waldo Emerson

"Where there is no vision the people perish."
Proverbs 29:18

The Outer Self
Dream-Fantasy

Dreams are
vague

Dreams seem
unobtainable

Sees problems
but not
solutions

THE REAL YOU
Dream-Purpose

Unstoppable
Confident
Holds a vision
Abundant
Soaring
Fulfilled
Accepts help from others
Committed
Confident in your knowing

Too proud
to accept
help

Settles
for
less

Procrastinates

Motivated by
selfishness

Your dream-fantasy exists in the outer self, where it will never become part of your reality because hindrances keep it from becoming your purpose in life.

Your dream-fantasy becomes a dream-purpose when you allow the real you to take control by changing your thoughts–every change in your life begins with a change in you.

Hold the Vision — Know You Were Born To Soar

Fascination is very powerful. You create a vision around those things which fascinate you. It starts as a seed and begins to grow. When you become totally fascinated with something, you become unstoppable. If a person becomes completely fascinated with becoming a doctor, then he will hold onto that vision even though it involves many years of training. He will work hard to get into medical school, and then spend a large amount of money to attend, believing it will all be worth it once he receives a degree. Although the entire process of becoming a doctor is extremely challenging, the fascination with his ultimate goal keeps him working toward it.

Remember, every person who creates something wonderful starts with a dream. A dream that you do not take seriously simply remains a fantasy, but a dream nurtured by the real you becomes your dream-purpose. When your dream becomes your purpose, it is no longer just an option. Therefore, you immediately begin to build a vision around your dream-purpose. Once you have built a vision of the steps you will need to take to make your dream a reality, then you become a person on a mission. **Your dream-purpose plus your vision equals your mission.**

In the diagram, you can see the distinction between a dream-fantasy and a dream-purpose. Your dream-fantasy exists in the outer self, where it never has a chance to become part of your reality. Hindrances such as procrastination and fear make it seem beyond your reach and, as a result, keep it from becoming your purpose in life. A dream-fantasy is vague; you never know exactly what you

93

are working toward because the edges are fuzzy and unclear. How can you reach a goal that you can't see?

Your dream-fantasy becomes a dream-purpose when you change your thoughts and allow the real you to be in control. Your dream-purpose becomes the driving force in your life and nothing will stop you from seeing it through. Rather than procrastinating or starting and stopping, you are propelled by faith and gain momentum along the way. You have a clear vision of your next level in life and there is no question in your mind as to whether you will reach that level — reaching it is inevitable.

Once you are on a mission, you become absolutely unstoppable. To build a vision, you must write down on paper the steps that will take you from where you are to where you want to be. This is your track on which to run, and this is the vision you will impart to other people who are involved in your mission with you. Each person will need to understand how this collective vision will enable his or her own personal mission to become a reality.

My parents were unable to have children. They went to several doctors for help, but each doctor said the same thing — if you want children, you will have to adopt because it is physically impossible for you to conceive a child. As a last resort, they decided to see a minister named William Branham. My parents had heard that Reverend Branham had a supernatural gift from God. He ministered to people and their otherwise incurable diseases were healed. Reverend Branham was holding a tent meeting about 150 miles from my parents' home, so they loaded their car with food and clothing for the trip and started down the highway. On their way they stopped at a rest area to use the restroom. When they came back to the car they discovered that all of their clothes and food had been stolen from the back seat. Determine to not let anything stop them they continued to drive toward the meeting.

They arrived at the tent meeting a few minutes after the service started. Although the tent was packed with several thousand people, they managed to find a seat. After Reverend Branham finished preaching the sermon, he bowed his head and prayed for all the people who had come to the service to ask God to heal them from sickness and disease. After the prayer, he looked up and pointed to my mother, who was seated in the audience. He asked her, "Woman do I know you?" She said, "No," then guided with this special gift he said "The doctors have told you that you can't have children and that you might as well adopt, isn't that right?" and she said "yes." Then Reverend Branham spoke these words: "In nine months, you will have a child." Guess what happened exactly nine months later? My mother had a child!

If at any point my parents would have stopped holding the vision they would not have ended up at the "right place, at the right time" to receive their breakthrough and begin having children. There are designated points on the road of life where you will come in contact with the exact right people, opportunities, and means of supply that are missing pieces to the puzzle. The only way you will find them is to keep moving forward. On days when you feel like you are "on a roll" you keep moving forward, on days when nothing seems to be going right you work on your thoughts to stay in the flow. Everyone and every thing you need is at some point up the road, but you have to keep taking action and moving forward to get there. There are times when everything on the outside will seem to contradict the vision that you are holding. As you continue to flow from the Real You, you are aware of the fact that "this to shall pass" You realize that what you are experiencing is nothing more than some turbulence that you must fly through to breakthrough to your next higher level.

Six months after I was born, my parents took me to another minister and told him I was a miracle and they wanted to dedicate me to God. The minister held me in his arms and said a short prayer of dedication. He then looked up at my parents and said, "Your son will grow up with a message burning in his heart. He will speak to crowds of tens of thousands of people."

For the first 17 years of my life, I did not look like anyone who even ten people would want to listen to. I put my mother through hell. Many nights I would come home at two or three o'clock in the morning and see the familiar sight of my mother kneeling by the sofa, tears streaming down her face and soaking the cushions of the couch. She would say, "God, please save my son. I don't know what he's doing out there so late, but if he keeps doing it, I know he won't live to see his twentieth birthday." I was a tough guy until I heard my mother crying, and then I would feel horrible. I would go into the living room and plead with her to stop crying. I would promise to change the next day, but the next day I would get up and do the same thing all over again. I felt out of control.

For years, she looked past my outward appearance to the person I was inside. She reminded me that I would grow up with a message burning in my heart and that I would speak to crowds of tens of thousands of people. My mother repeated that same vision to me every chance she got. In 1978, a month before my mom died, I spoke publicly for the first time. My mother was sitting in the front row.

Hold The Vision

For years I spoke anywhere and everywhere, but to speak to a crowd of ten thousand people in one building was still more than I could imagine. Then in May of 1994 I was sitting in my office at two o'clock in the morning. I had just returned from speaking at the Yager Weekend of the Diamonds. It was held in Greensboro, North Carolina, where 16,000 people packed the Greensboro Coliseum. As I sat behind my desk trying to work, a thought crossed my mind, shaking me to the core of my being. I realized that the words spoken to my parents when I was six months old had just come to pass.

If you will bring your dream from the outside into the real you and build a vision around that dream, then you will become a man or woman on a mission, flying to the heights of achievement, prosperity, and fulfillment.

One day while talking on the phone with a dear friend, he said, "You know Larry, when I started my business thirty years ago, I never dreamed my family and I would live as well as we do. I never focused on just acquiring money, though. I focused on the good things money could be used for." He built a vision around that principle. He set out on a mission, and the mission became his reality and created his lifestyle.

You must hold your vision and know it like you know your name. Can you imagine someone trying to convince you that your name is not really your name, or that you cannot use your name anymore? If someone wanted me to believe that, I would probably just think to myself, *oh, you poor misguided soul. I have had this name for 42 years. You must not be thinking right.* You must hold your vision so strongly that when someone tries to talk you out of it, you look at them as if they are crazy. As you hold your vision, you will find that the people who do not believe in your dream will not want to be around you as much. Instead, people who have their own vision and mission in life will seek your company.

The fact that you never go to a higher level without the help of others is a principle you will quickly learn. You will always have someone helping you, and you will always have the opportunity to help someone else at the same time. When you are flowing from the real you, you will become a great artist. I am not talking about using a paintbrush, though. For people to join and assist you with your vision, you must become an artist of words. You must paint a picture with words which will inspire and attract others. They will want to be a part of your business, to buy what you are selling, or to join your cause or mission. You can paint a picture with words that will arouse interest in your children and influence them to be a part of your mission.

A solid commitment to your daily program of books, tapes, and positive conversations becomes especially important when dealing with other people. When you change your thoughts, philosophy, reality, and life, you will become a better artist and attract the right kind of people to you. Your outer self is motivated by selfishness, but the real you is a magnet that attracts the highest and best. As you focus on your vision, you are attracting your dream like a magnet. When you attract your dream, you receive what is good for you. You attract that which already had your name on it and which belonged to you all along.

Everything it takes to make your dream a reality already has your name on it, but it is up to you to focus on the desires of the real you so you can attract your dream-purpose to you.

The entire process of owning your dream is similar to pregnancy. Men and women both can personally experience this kind of pregnancy. The seed of a thought is planted in the womb of the real you and conception takes place. Then the dream-thought begins to grow and develop. Your dream grows inside you before anyone else can see it. Finally, after the dream is ready for birth, there is labor and delivery. Your dream manifests itself where everyone can see it.

Work Through Challenges – They're only Temporary

When circumstances challenge you, you must strive to remain true to who you really are more than ever. Hold a vision of your life in your mind and stay focused, even if everything on the outside contradicts your dream. At times you may be tempted to quit and people may call you crazy, but keep holding the vision.

You become like the marathon runner who hits the "wall" after running for miles. Every nerve in her body screams out in pain. . Her mind is telling her to quit, saying, *What good is it if you die running this marathon?* But no matter how much it hurts or what her mind says, she must remember to concentrate on two things. First, she must remember that the pain is only temporary. Just about everything in life is temporary. Most obstacles that stop people are short-lived. If you keep holding the vision, you will get through it. Second, she must remember that the worst thing to do is stop running. I have talked to several marathon runners and they all say the same thing — if you stop when you hit the "wall" you will stay in pain. But if you keep running, if you keep holding the vision, you will reach that wonderful moment when you break through the "wall" and experience a rush of endorphins throughout your entire body that eases the pain. The last few miles of the marathon are easier than the first few because you are experiencing what is called the "runner's high." The last phases of your mission will come more easily once you have met all the challenges along the way. **Hold the vision**. Focus your mental ability. Attract your dream.

Imagine a little deer running through the woods, panting. Her throat is dry and parched. Her tongue is sticking to the roof of her mouth. She knows she must find water soon or she will collapse from exhaustion and dehydration. Since she has never been in this part of the woods before, she does not know where water is from memory or past experience. Then all of a sudden, instinctively, she knows there is water to the north. She turns and begins to run with all her might in that direction.

If you could communicate with the deer you could ask where she is going, and she would say she was going to the brook to drink water. If you ask if she has ever been to the brook before, or if she's familiar with that area of the woods, or if she is able to hear the water, she would have to answer no to all of those questions. The natural question to ask next is how she knows the water is in that direction, to which she would reply, "I know it's there because I know it's there."

As you flow more and more from the real you, you will just know some things. When people ask you how you know you are going to reach your higher level, the only answer you may have is, "I know because I know." If you are alive, then you have a dream to live. Someone once said that most people die at age 25, they just don't get buried until they are 70 or 80 years old. You "die" inside when you choose to ignore and refuse to act on your dreams.

I would like to end this book with a story which has meant a lot to me over the past few years:

A little boy was walking through a field one day. He saw the sun reflect off of something that was white in color and was laying in the tall grass. Pushing the grass aside, he discovered it was an egg. Since it was larger than the chicken eggs back in the barn, he assumed it must have come from a very large chicken. He took it back to the chicken coop, lifted one of the mother hens, and carefully placed the egg next to the others on which she was sitting. After some time had passed, all the eggs began to crack open. Several baby chicks poked their little heads out of their eggs. Then the larger egg cracked open, but it was not a chick at all. Out popped the head of a baby eaglet!

The eaglet looked around with curiosity at the world into which he had been born. After a short time, he noticed that his stomach hurt and felt empty. He looked around and saw that the way the others around him alleviated this stomach pain was to pick around in the dirt and gravel until they found enough food to fill their stomachs. He noticed they communicated with each other by saying "ba-bwak ba-bwak ba-bwak," and that they had wings on their sides like he did. The chicks would fly two feet off the ground and land seven feet across the chicken yard. The baby eaglet thought to himself, *Well, I guess that is better than walking.* But each day as he had his face in the dirt looking for food, as he learned to talk like a chicken, and as he used his powerful wings to fly only seven feet across the yard, dropping to the ground before hitting the fence, he thought, *This just doesn't feel right.* Something inside of him was telling him there must be something more to life than this. But every time he would get frustrated and begin to dream about something greater, he would look around at the chickens and think, *No, this is reality. I had better settle down and accept life for what it is and forget about these crazy dreams.*

In the meantime, the baby eaglet's mother had been scouring the countryside for two weeks looking for her missing baby. On the fourteenth day, she flew over the chickenyard and spotted the baby eaglet. She realized the eaglet looked like one of her own, so she took another lap around the chickenyard to get a closer look. As she focused even more, she recognized the baby eaglet's eyes and realized it was her son. She let out a sharp yell. As the powerful screech hit the chickenyard, all of the chickens and roosters looked up and saw the eagle, commenting on the eagle's stupidity and saying that, if they tried to fly that high, they would fall and break their necks.

The baby eaglet, however, looked up at its beautiful mother and thought, *Yes! I knew I wasn't born to bury my face in the dirt in search of food, or to talk this chicken talk, or to use these powerful wings only to fly across the chickenyard. I was born to soar!* And with a few flaps of his wings, he was up in the sky soaring to the heavens with his mother.

This story illustrates beautifully the difference between settling for less and living your dreams. The baby eaglet's entire life had been lived with chickens as role models. Even though the eaglet knew something in his life was not fulfilling, he dismissed his inner voice as crazy and allowed himself to be bogged down by the realities of the chickenyard. Although it did not feel right, he settled for "flying" like the chickens, allowing his powerful wings to go to waste.

When you are not flowing from the real you, you are much like the baby eaglet living with the chickens. The circumstances of your life are unfulfilling and you know there is something greater for you, a higher level to live on. The person who lives on the inside is your true identity. The dream that calls you is the real destiny for your life. You have to be willing to answer the call if you want to own your dreams and soar. **Your dream-purpose is calling to you. Say "Yes!"**

<u>A NOTE FROM LARRY DiANGI:</u>

Dear Friend,

In future books I will be including letters from people who are using the Purpose Driven principles in this book to create breakthroughs in their personal and professional lives.

Please send me your letter explaining what the message in this book has meant to you and how you are using these principles to overcome challenges and PURSUE YOUR PURPOSE WITH A PASSION.

My mailing address is: Larry DiAngi, PO Box 9056, Erie, PA, 16505, USA.
www.larrydiangi.com

Thank You... I look forward to hearing from you.

Yours On Purpose,
Larry

To book Larry DiAngi to speak
at your event or function, please call:
800-690-1372
www.larrydiangi.com

You can take the next step and a quantum leap to living a Purpose-Driven life by receiving Larry DiAngi's latest six tape series entitled:

OWN YOUR DREAM–
THE RESILIENT POWER OF PURPOSE

If you want to continue your journey of becoming Purpose-Driven in every area of your life; than this six tape series is for you. Included are dynamic recordings from Larry's live seminars and inspiring studio recordings, plus a Journal/Manual. Throughout this series Larry coaches you and gives you breakthrough strategies for staying On Purpose, flowing from the Real You, and attracting your best in life...

TO ORDER PLEASE CALL:

800-690-1372
www.larrydiangi.com

About The Author

Larry DiAngi is living proof that the principles he shares will work if you "work them". He delivers keynote speeches and conducts seminars for both business and public audiences around the world.

During his early years it seemed unlikely that he would do anything significant in life. Then at age 17 he began a relentless study of individuals who had found purpose, meaning and success. This pursuit developed into a passion to share what he was learning with others.

His experiences in life and constant quest for principles that produce real results, prepared him to share these principles with people from all walks of life. From playing drums in rock bands, to shop work on an assembly line, then sold fire extinguishers door to door to businesses, spent time in the ministry, a staff counselor at a home for juvenile delinquents, was sales director for a local magazine, then president of a corporation. For years he also hosted a weekly television show on an ABC affiliate and a daily radio program. Larry moved on to speak to audiences nationally and internationally as he has continued to do for the past ten years. He has become a sought after resource for personal and professional development.

Larry's mission is to give people principles that will help them discover and live from the inspiration of their purpose, create breakthroughs, and go on to make their dreams a reality.

NOTES

NOTES